I0820329

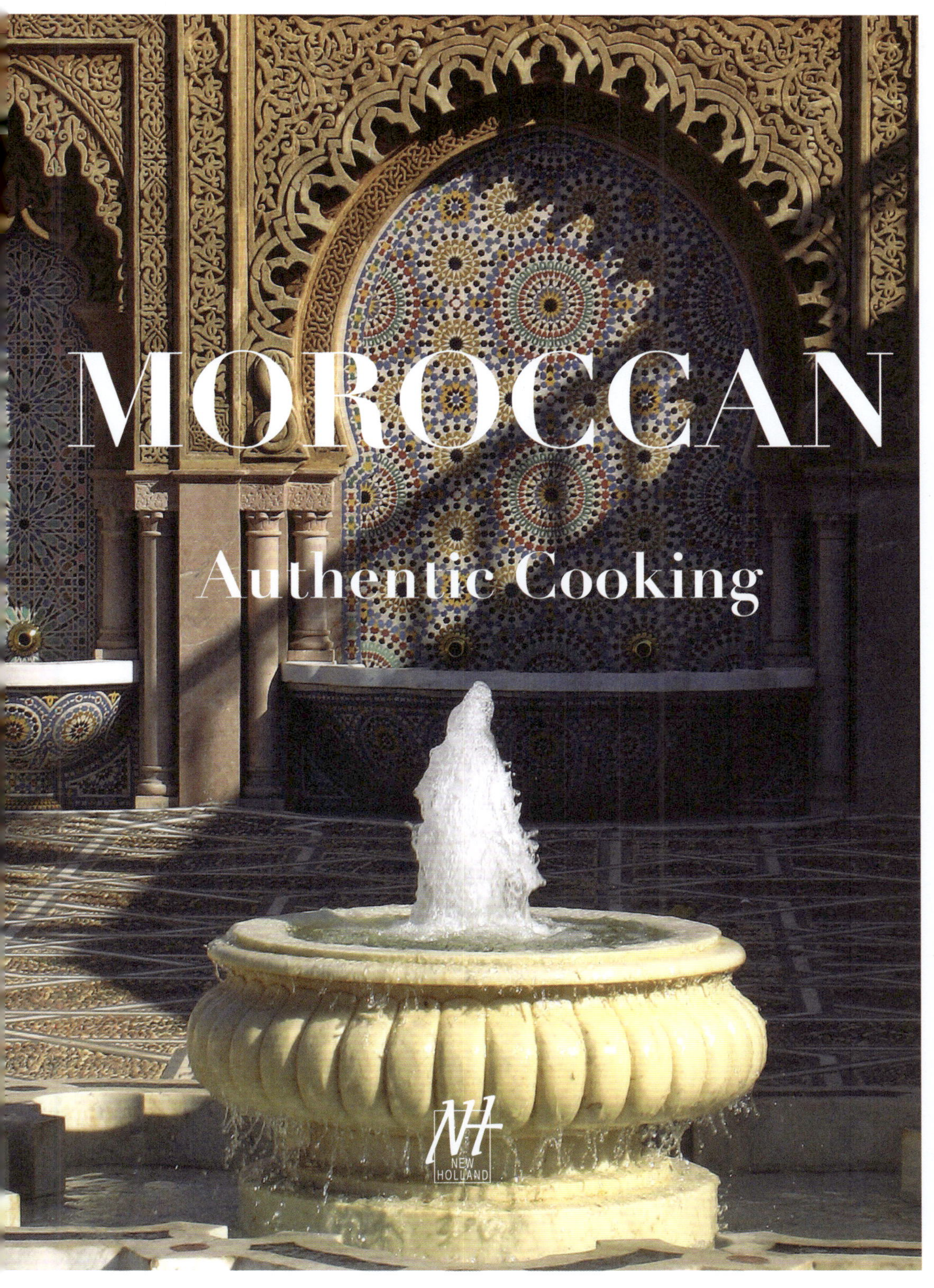

MOROCCAN

Authentic Cooking

NH
NEW HOLLAND

Contents

Introduction

Morocco, officially the Kingdom of Morocco, is in North West Africa and is bordered by the Mediterranean Sea to the north, the Atlantic Ocean to the west, Mauritania (which lies beyond the disputed territory of Western Sahara) to the south, and Algeria to the east. Principal cities include Rabat (the capital), Casablanca, Marrakech and Fes.

The Atlas Mountains, rising to 4,167 metres in Jebel Toubkal in the southwest, dominate most of the country. In the south lie the sandy wastes of the Sahara desert, but in the north is a fertile coastal plain, home of most of the population. Agriculture and mining are economic mainstays. Morocco is a leading producer and exporter of phosphates, and other important minerals include iron ore, copper, lead, zinc, cobalt, manganese and coal. Food processing and the manufacture of leather goods and textiles are also important. Half the labour force is employed in agriculture, growing cereals, citrus fruits and vegetables. Tourism and fishing also contribute to the economy.

Most Moroccans are of mixed Arab–Berber descent and are Muslim – although Islam is the state religion, there are small Christian and Jewish minorities. Arabic is the official language, but Berber dialects, French (a main language of commerce) and Spanish are also spoken.

THE LAND AND ITS PEOPLE

CAPITAL	Rabat
LARGEST CITY	Casablanca
AREA	445,050 sq km
POPULATION	31,500,000
LANGUAGE	Arabic
ETHNIC GROUPS	Arab/Berber (99.1%), Jewish (0.2%), other (0.7%)
RELIGION	Muslim (98.7%), Christian (1.1%), Jewish (0.2%)
CURRENCY	Moroccan dirham (MAD)
NATIONAL DAY	March 2nd (Independence Day)

History

Originally inhabited by Berbers, Morocco became a province of the Roman Empire in the 1st century AD. After successive invasions by barbarian tribes, Islam was brought by the Arabs in 685. An independent Moroccan kingdom was established in 788, and its dissolution in the 10th century began a period of anarchy. The country was finally united in the 11th century by the Almoravids, a Berber-Muslim dynasty, who established a kingdom reaching from Spain to Senegal.

Unity was never complete, however, and conflict between Arabs and Berbers was incessant. European encroachment began in 1415, when Portugal captured Ceuta, and ended with the Portuguese defeat at the battle of Ksar el Kebir (Alcazarquivir) in 1578. In the 19th and early 20th centuries the strategic importance and economic potential of Morocco once again excited the European powers, sparking an intense, often violent, rivalry among France, Spain and Germany.

Finally, in 1912, most of Morocco became a French protectorate, while a small area became a Spanish protectorate. Nationalist feelings began to surface in the 1930s, becoming more militant after World War II, and in 1956 Morocco gained its independence.

In 1957 the sultan became King Muhammad V. He was succeeded in 1961 by his son, Hassan II, whose early reign, plagued by internal unrest, coups and assassination attempts, was repressive.

Hassan's position was strengthened in 1976 when Spain relinquished the Spanish Sahara (now Western Sahara) to joint Moroccan–Mauritanian control. Challenged by the Polisario Front, a guerrilla movement backed by Algeria and seeking independence for the area, Mauritania withdrew in 1979, but Morocco continued battling there and claimed the entire territory. King Hassan died in 1999 and was succeeded by his son Muhammad VI.

Most Moroccans today can claim both Berber and Arab ancestry, though they are generally referred to as Berbers. There is a small amount that can claim pure Arab decent and a few small groups of true Berbers that still exist in the Rif Mountains, Atlas Mountains and Souss Valley and who are able to speak several ancient Berber languages. There is also a small number of Jews and black African Moroccans.

The population of Morocco numbers over 30 million people and many of them are not well off. Lifestyles differ depending on the areas that people live in. People living in rural areas are often unable to get fairly basic items, classed as everyday items in most cultures. They generally tend to grow plants or tend livestock for food. However there are far greater clusters of people in the cities, which bustle with life at all times of the day. Souks (markets) are virtually a way of life for most Moroccans and can be found in every town and city. The majority of souks, however, are closed during the lunch period and on Fridays. Most Moroccans are friendly and hospitable and will extend warm invitations if you do not act rudely or unfriendly towards them.

The rich culture and diversity of Morocco is reflected in every face of this vibrant nation. These people have a long and fascinating heritage and, though they've slowly started to embrace the modernizing of their world, there is a sort of timelessness that still hangs over them all.

Moroccan Houses

The roof is a centre of everyday life for Moroccan families. Almost every house in Morocco has a roof that is constructed as a terrace.

On the roof, not only the laundry is washed and hung to dry, but the women also receive their friends here or hold a small talk with the neighbours. The terrace is often furnished comfortably with chairs and tables. Sometimes a part of the roof also serves as a chicken-house or temporary abode for sheep before the great holidays.

Women and children in smaller cities and rural regions spend a large part of their day on the roof-terrace. There, they are sheltered and can get fresh air at the same time. The Moroccan film maker Farida Ben Lyziad describes the former social function of the roof: the streets were reserved for the men, the rooves belonged to the women.

In summer, when the house is too hot, the whole family often sleeps on the roof in the cool night air. If you have the chance to be invited to a Moroccan house you should not miss spending some time on the roof and enjoying the fresh breeze.

Another very important part of the Moroccan house or apartment is the salon. Here, in the best room, visitors are received and large festivities and family reunions are held. Every Moroccan regards it as the centre of hospitality and social life, and its decorations are its owner's pride and joy.

In some houses, especially large ones, the salon is a room or even a hall of its own. In others, it's part the living room. Whether small or large, they all have a certain structure in common. Along the walls there are sofas or comfortably cushioned and padded benches with a backrest, coated with expensive fabrics. The little tables in front of the benches or sofas are often beautifully ornate and serve for setting down the tea and sweets. The walls are decorated, usually with the traditional zellije (hand-cut tile) ornaments. But there are also more European-style wall decorations, depending on the owner's preference and taste.

The coverings are changed every few years, sometimes even every year. There are special shops that sell fabrics and cushions for the salon. Especially in the large cities like Casablanca, Rabat or Fes you can have a great time window-shopping for interior decoration! It's just a pity all those beautiful fabrics and cushions are too heavy for the plane!

Daily Life in Morocco

One of the best ways to dive into Moroccan culture is to strike up a conversation with the person sitting next to you at a local cafe. A simple conversation over a warm cup of sweet coffee could lead to a lifelong friendship long after you leave Morocco.

By nature, Moroccan people are hospitable – it is an essential element to their culture. At first, they can seem intimidating and unapproachable. All it takes is an open mind and friendly nature to become fast friends with anyone from Morocco.

This might lead to your new friend extending an invitation to enjoy a Moroccan meal at their home. What better opportunity to savour the delicious Moroccan cuisine? There are a few items of respect to keep in mind before entering someone's home, however. A respected cultural practice is to remove shoes before entering a Moroccan home. As you would at home when invited to a friend's for dinner, bring a gift along, such as a dessert of kaab el ghzal, ghriba or briouates (almond paste cookie,

almond-sugar cookie, and fried-cheese pastry, respectively). If you're eating in the countryside, however, you might consider bringing over a chicken or meat product to add to the menu.

Once inside the home, there is a certain dining practice to keep in mind. Moroccan people use their hands like Westerners use utensils during meals. A slice of bread functions as a spoon or fork as well. Your dinner host will expect you to follow this practice. Asking for other utensils or not following the practice will appear disrespectful. Keep in mind when using hands as a utensil that Moroccan practice is to eat only with the right hand – the left hand is for restroom business.

Many Moroccan women are not typically on the streets of Morocco, but are often at home preparing food for the next family meal. However, in the larger, more urban settings of Marrakech, Rabat,

or Casablanca these conventions are slowly changing. When a woman visiting Morocco makes a new friend, that friend may invite her over for a cup of tea or a hamman, a Moroccan bath.

Before snapping a picture of a Moroccan person or scenic background that a Moroccan person may appear in, ask permission first. Doing anything less is offensive, so much so that the person may request money for that picture of a tree or scenic overlook featured behind them. The only exception to this practice is when you have an established relationship with a Moroccan person. In fact, your new Moroccan friend may well bring you to an ideal photographic location or request a copy of the photograph as a special memento of your friendship. In Morocco, you'll have plenty of friends in no time!

Moroccan Food

Moroccan cuisine is very diverse, with many influences. The reason for this is centuries of interaction between Morocco and the outside world. The cuisine of Morocco is a mix of Arab, Berber, Moorish, Middle Eastern, Mediterranean, African and other influences. The cooks in the royal kitchens of Fes, Meknes, Marrakech, Rabat and Tetouan refined their best over the centuries and created the basis for what is known as Moroccan cuisine today.

Moroccan food is one of the most cleverly balanced cuisines on earth. Spices are used to enhance the flavour of dishes and there is nothing like the warm waft of beautiful spices that seduce you when you open the lid of a tagine. The essence of Moroccan food is a communal style of eating, with many dishes shared by the family. The meal-time is very social and eaten at a leisurely pace with much laughter and talking.

When entering a Moroccan home, you would be offered food and usually tea within a heartbeat. Hospitality is a very important part of Moroccan culture and making guests welcome is also part of Islamic teaching.

Spices are used extensively in Moroccan food. While spices have been imported to Morocco for thousands of years, many ingredients, like saffron from Tiliouine, mint and olives from Meknes, and oranges and lemons from Fes, are home-grown.

Common spices include karfa (cinnamon), kamoun (cumin), kharkoum (turmeric), skingbir (ginger), libzar (pepper), tahmira (paprika), anise seed, sesame seed, kasbour (coriander), maadnous (parsley), zaafrane beldi (saffron) and mint. At the street market or in the elaborately stocked spice shops, the ras el hanout (head of the shop) has his own particular blend of spices, which can contain a mixture of anywhere from 10 to 100 spices. Each vendor has his own secret recipe and no two are exactly alike, as they are often secretly handed down through the family for many generations.

40
CURCUMIN
40
PAPRIKA
40
CORIANDRE
70
GINGEMBRE
70

fenugreek seed
saffron
turmeric
cumin seed
sesame seed
anise seed
pepper
cardamom
coriander seed
bay leaves
ginger
mint

The midday meal is the main meal, with the exception of the holy month of Ramadan. The typical formal meal begins with a series of hot and cold salads, followed by a tagine. Bread is eaten with every meal. Often a lamb is cooked until so tender it can be pulled apart and eaten with the fingers. Chicken dishes normally follow red meat and then couscous topped with vegetables. A cup of sweet mint tea is next and is commonly used to end the meal.

The main Moroccan dish most people are familiar with is couscous (granular semolina), an old delicacy probably of Berber origin. It is often cooked with spices, vegetables, nuts and raisins. It makes a meal in itself or is topped with rich stews and roasted meats to make a more complete meal.

Beef is the most commonly eaten red meat in Morocco. Lamb is preferred, but is not as common due to its higher cost. Poultry was historically used, and the importance of seafood is increasing in Moroccan food. The breed of sheep in North Africa has much of its fat concentrated in its tail, which means that Moroccan lamb does not have the pungent flavour that Western lamb and mutton can have.

Among the most famous Moroccan dishes are couscous, pastilla (also spelled bsteeya or bastilla), tagine, tanjia and harira. Although the latter is a soup, it is considered as a dish in itself and is served as such or with dates, especially during the month of Ramadan.

The most common cooking utensil is the tagine – an earthenware pot with a lid that assists the cooking, much the same way as a slow cooker.

Sweets are not usually served at the end of a Moroccan meal, but seasonal fruits are common. A typical dessert is kaab el ghzal (gazelle's horns), which is a pastry stuffed with almond paste and topped with sugar. Another dessert is halwa shebakia, which is essentially pretzel-shaped pieces of dough deep-fried and dipped into a hot pot of honey and sprinkled with sesame seeds. Halwa shebakia are also eaten during the month of Ramadan. Zucre coco are coconut fudge cakes that are also popular.

Moroccan Tea Culture

The most popular drink in Morocco is green tea with mint. Traditionally, making good mint tea is considered an art form, and the drinking of it with friends and family members is one of the important rituals of the day. The technique of pouring the tea is as crucial as the quality of the tea. The tea is accompanied with hard sugar cones or lumps.

Moroccan tea pots have long, curved pouring spouts and this allows the tea to be poured evenly into tiny glasses from a height. To acquire the optimum taste, glasses are filled in two stages. Moroccans traditionally like tea with bubbles, so while pouring they hold the teapot high above the glasses.

Tea is sold all around the country for 2–3 dirhams per cup, although it is often served free when you are negotiating a purchase. You can also buy it as loose tea from all kinds of markets around the country.

Selling fast food in the street has long been a tradition, and the best example is Djemaa el Fna square in Marrakech. Starting in the 1980s, new snack restaurants started serving bocadillo (which is a Spanish word for a sandwich, widely used in Morocco). Though the composition of a bocadillo varies by region, usually the bocadillo is a baguette filled with salad and a choice of meats, fish (usually tuna) or a dense egg omelette.

Dairy products are widely available throughout Morocco in shops known as mahlaba. While offering all types of dairy products, mahlaba often sell juices and breakfasts as well as bocadillos, competing with formerly established snack restaurants.

The late 1990s also saw the opening of franchises of multinational fast food chains, especially in major cities.

The Art of Moroccan Cooking

- Ensure that you have a sufficient range of herbs and spices before attempting any of these recipes
- It's a good idea to have a medium-sized earthenware tagine as one of your major Moroccan utensils
- The focal point of Moroccan hospitality is tea – ensure you have quality tea on hand

Snacks & Starters

Most meals begin with a simple selection of mezze, which might include a bowl of olives or a selection of cooked vegetable salads dressed with olive oil, sprinkled with cumin and served with flat bread.
We have selected a broad range of recipes in this chapter guaranteed to tempt the tastebuds. You will find the various herbs and spices used will definitely attract you to the tastes of Morocco.

SERVES 4

Simple Harissa

PREPARATION 10 mins

4 fresh red chillies, chopped
1 large clove garlic, crushed
1 teaspoon ground cumin
½ teaspoon ground coriander
1 tablespoon olive oil

1 Mix all ingredients together well. Serve in a small bowl at the table as a condiment, or add about a teaspoonful to soups and stews.

NOTE This version of harissa is quick and convenient. Store covered in the refrigerator – will keep for many weeks.

SERVES 6

Rose Water Candied Peanuts

PREPARATION 15 mins COOKING 35 mins

¾ cup sugar
1¾ cups dry-roasted peanuts
¼ teaspoon salt
1½ teaspoons rose water

1 Line a baking tray with foil. Bring sugar and ¼ cup water to the boil in a 3-litre heavy saucepan over moderate heat, stirring until sugar is dissolved.

2 Stir in peanuts and boil, stirring frequently, until syrup thickens, about 8 minutes. Reduce heat to moderately low and stir in the salt. Continue cooking, stirring and scraping any bits of crystallised sugar from side of pan into mixture (it will become very gritty) until sugar is golden brown, about 2–3 minutes more. The sugar will still be gritty.

3 Remove from heat and stir in rose water. Spread nuts on foil to cool completely.

MAKES 16

Moroccan Flat Bread

PREPARATION 25 mins **COOKING** 1 hr 20 mins

- 450g stone-ground wholemeal flour
- ¾ teaspoon paprika
- ½ teaspoon salt
- ½ teaspoon dried yeast
- 1 teaspoon sugar
- 1 tablespoon olive oil
- 3 tablespoons sesame seeds
- 1 egg, lightly beaten

1 Sift the flour, paprika and salt together into a large bowl. Make a deep well in the centre and pour in ⅓ cup tepid water. Add the yeast and sugar, stir lightly to dissolve. Bubbles should appear, showing the yeast is active. Pour in 1 cup tepid water and the oil. With a wooden spoon, commence stirring from the centre out, taking in flour gradually as you stir. Continue with your hand as it gets heavy, and form a dough.

2 Turn dough out onto a lightly floured surface. Knead for 8–10 minutes, sprinkling surface with a little flour if it sticks, until dough is smooth and elastic to touch.

3 Place in a clean lightly oiled bowl, cover with cling wrap and leave to rise in a warm place for 30–40 minutes or until it doubles in size. With your fist, punch the centre of the dough once, to release air, and turn out onto lightly floured surface. Knead for 2 minutes then shape into an even log. Cut into 16 even pieces.

4 Roll out each piece into a 7cm circle and place onto a tea towel in a single layer, cover with another towel and leave to rise 15 minutes. Preheat the oven to 150°C and lightly butter 3 oven trays. Place sesame seeds on a small plate, shake plate twice so seeds will be in single layer. Have beaten egg and brush ready.

5 Brush 1 flat bread with a good coating of egg then lift and place egg-side down onto the sesame seeds, press lightly, then lift onto the oven tray, seed-side up. Re-sprinkle the plate with sesame seeds and repeat process with remaining dough. When first tray is full, place in oven and bake for 15 minutes, then continue with remaining trays – it is best to cook 1 tray at a time on centre shelf. Remove to a cooling rack to cool so base will remain crisp. Store in an airtight tin when cooled.

NOTE Ordinary wholemeal flour may also be used, or use half white, half wholemeal.

SERVES 6

Carrot Dip

PREPARATION 5 mins

1 carrot, peeled
1 clove garlic
½ cup natural yoghurt
pinch of salt
6 olives, chopped

1 Cut the carrot into a few chunks and put in the food processor along with the clove of garlic. Process for about 1 minute. Transfer to a bowl.

2 Add the yoghurt and salt and mix. Garnish with chopped olives. Sprinkle with cumin seeds if you wish. Serve with crusty bread slices.

SERVES 10

Moroccan Spiced Olives

PREPARATION 10 mins COOKING 2 mins

1 tablespoon olive oil
1 teaspoon cumin seeds
1 teaspoon fennel seeds
1 teaspoon coriander seeds
¼ teaspoon ground cardamom
pinch of ground nutmeg
pinch of ground cinnamon
1½ cups green olives
1 tablespoon lemon juice
1 tablespoon orange juice
3 cloves garlic, minced

1 Heat olive oil, cumin seeds, fennel seeds, coriander seeds, cardamom, nutmeg and cinnamon in a saucepan over medium heat until fragrant, about 2 minutes.

2 Remove from heat, add olives and toss to coat. Stir in remaining ingredients. Refrigerate in an airtight container for at least 4 hours or up to 3 weeks.

3 Drain and serve at room temperature.

SERVES 4

Peasant Pancakes

PREPARATION 15 mins COOKING 5 mins

4 bananas, peeled
½ cup apricot liqueur
1 cup pancake mix
vegetable oil for frying
½ cup soft breadcrumbs
45g butter, melted
4 tablespoons sugar
1 teaspoon ground ginger

1 Cut the bananas into 1cm slices and place in a bowl. Add apricot liqueur and marinate for ½ hour.

2 In another bowl, place the pancake mix. Follow package directions to make thick pancake batter, using the apricot liqueur drained from the bananas as part of the liquid.

3 Add bananas to the batter and stir thoroughly. In a large, heavy-based frying pan, add 1cm cooking oil. Drop the mixture by tablespoonfuls (2 or 3 pieces of banana in each spoon) into the hot fat until golden brown on both sides. Remove and set aside.

4 Combine the soft breadcrumbs, melted butter, sugar and ground ginger. Place pancakes on dessert plates and sprinkle 1–2 tablespoons breadcrumb mixture on the pancakes to serve.

NOTE Crystallised ginger may be used instead of ground ginger, in which case use 2 tablespoons sugar and 2 tablespoons crystallised ginger, minced finely.

SERVES 4

Orange Nut Couscous

PREPARATION 20 mins COOKING 15 mins

1 tablespoon olive oil
1 cup almonds, coarsely chopped
1 onion, chopped
½ green capsicum, chopped
2 cups orange juice
2 cinnamon sticks
5 cloves
¼ teaspoon turmeric
¼ teaspoon paprika
¼ teaspoon salt
¼ teaspoon pepper
2 cups couscous
¼ cup raisins
2 green onions, chopped

1 Heat oil in a large frying pan and cook almonds until lightly toasted.

2 Add onion and green capsicum and cook until soft. Add orange juice, cinnamon, cloves and spices and bring to the boil.

3 Quickly stir in couscous and raisins, then cover and turn off heat. Let stand for 5 minutes or until liquid is absorbed completely.

4 Fluff with a fork before serving. Sprinkle each portion with green onions.

SERVES 6

Honeyed Red Onion Confit

PREPARATION 15 mins   COOKING 30 mins

3 tablespoons vegetable oil
1 kg red onions, halved lengthwise, then thinly sliced
1 cup sultanas
½ cup honey
1½ teaspoons ground ginger
1¼ teaspoons ground cinnamon

1 Heat oil in a 3-litre heavy saucepan over moderate heat until hot but not smoking, then cook onions, stirring occasionally, until they begin to soften, about 7 minutes.

2 Add sultanas, honey, ginger and cinnamon and cook, uncovered, stirring occasionally until onions are very tender and slightly caramelised, about 20–25 minutes. Serve with Moroccan Spiced Pork or Veal Couscous Casserole.

NOTE Confit can be made 1 week ahead, then covered and chilled. Reheat to warm before serving.

SERVES 8

Preserved Lemons

PREPARATION 30 mins **COOKING** 5 mins

3 good-quality fresh lemons, at room temperature
3 tablespoons salt

1 Wash lemons well, cut a slice from top and base to even off. Cut lemons in half lengthwise then cut each half into 4 wedges.

2 Place on a board and cut away the white core (pith). With a sharp knife, cut the flesh from the wedge down to the pith line and reserve.

3 Pack the wedge-shaped skins lightly into a jar.

4 Remove the seeds from the lemon flesh and place the flesh into a food processor or blender bowl. Add the salt and process until the lemon flesh is pulverised. Pour into the jar to surround and cover the lemon rind.

5 Place the jar in the microwave on high power for 4 minutes. Remove the jar from the oven and, when steam subsides, screw on the lid. Shake or turn jar around so juice is dispersed and place in a dark cupboard.

6 After 3 days the lemon rind will be ready for use. The pith will look translucent and the preserved lemon will be soft to the bite. After opening, store in the refrigerator.

7 To use, remove the amount needed, leaving the pulpy juice in the jar. Rinse the lemon well and cut into strips or dice as recipe instructs.

NOTE This is a quick method of preserving lemons, which departs from the traditional method but the result is the same. This method allows you to make 2 to 3 lemons at a time. A 350 mL jar will take 2 lemons filled to the top – 3 lemons need a larger jar. If there is a space at the top, float a little oil on the surface before placing on the lid.

MAKES THREE 20CM ROUNDS

Berber Soft Bread

PREPARATION 30 mins   COOKING 15 mins

3½ cups plain flour
1¼ teaspoons salt
½ cup vegetable oil
2 tablespoons honey

1 Mix flour and salt in food processor. Add 1 cup hot water and 4 tablespoons oil and blend until ball forms. Remove dough from processor.

2 Using oiled hands, divide dough into 3 equal pieces. Roll each piece on lightly floured surface until 20cm round and about 6mm thick.

3 Heat 1 tablespoon oil in a 25cm non-stick frying pan over medium heat.

4 Add 1 dough round to frying pan, reduce heat to medium-low and cook until golden on bottom, about 5 minutes.

5 Turn bread over and cook until golden on bottom and bread is cooked through, about 5 minutes. Transfer bread to plate.

6 Tent with foil to keep warm. Repeat with remaining oil and dough. Break warm bread into pieces, drizzle with honey and serve.

SERVES 5

Plain Couscous

PREPARATION 2 mins   COOKING 5 mins

¼ teaspoon salt
2½ cups couscous
60g butter
¼ cup olive oil

1 Bring 2½ cups water to the boil, add salt, couscous, butter and oil.

2 Stir until all liquid has been absorbed by couscous.

Soups

Harira is eaten all over Morocco. Though this hearty, bean-based soup (a meal in itself when eaten with some good bread) is traditionally used to break the Ramadan fasts, it's a dish eaten all year round. While harira is often flavoured with a little lamb or chicken, it's the humble legumes that are really the stars, so making a delicious vegetarian soup is very easy.

SERVES 6

Pumpkin and Chickpea Soup

PREPARATION 40 mins   COOKING 60 mins

2 cloves garlic
750g butternut pumpkin, peeled and cut into pieces 4cm thick
8 sprigs fresh thyme
2 tablespoons olive oil
1 leek
5cm piece ginger, peeled and finely chopped
2 x 400g canned chickpeas, rinsed and drained
1 carrot, peeled and diced
8 cups vegetable stock
¼ cup parsley, chopped

1 Preheat oven to 200°C. Place garlic, with skin intact, into a roasting tray with pumpkin. Scatter thyme over the pumpkin and drizzle with 1 tablespoon of olive oil. Cover loosely with foil and bake for 30 minutes.

2 Make an incision in the leek with a knife halfway through from top to bottom. Open the leek slightly, wash thoroughly, then slice thinly. Place the leek into a heavy-based saucepan with the remaining olive oil and fry over a low heat until soft and translucent.

3 Squeeze the garlic into the saucepan and add the roasted pumpkin, ginger, chickpeas, carrot and vegetable stock. Bring to the boil with the lid on. Reduce heat and simmer for 20 minutes. Serve garnished with parsley.

SERVES 6

Spiced Fish, Tomato and Chickpea Soup

PREPARATION 40 mins COOKING 40 mins

- 1 tablespoon olive oil
- 1 onion, chopped
- 1 teaspoon ground coriander
- 1 teaspoon ground cumin
- 1 teaspoon allspice
- 1 green chilli, finely sliced
- 400g canned chopped tomatoes
- 400g canned chickpeas, rinsed and drained
- 1 litre reduced-salt fish stock
- 500g firm white fish fillets such as redfish, bream or sea perch, cut into large pieces
- ⅓ cup couscous
- ½ cup natural yoghurt
- ¼ cup fresh parsley, chopped
- ¼ cup fresh mint, chopped

1 Heat the oil in a large pot, add the onion and cook over a medium heat for 3 minutes or until soft and golden.

2 Add the spices and chilli and cook until fragrant, about 2 minutes. Stir in the tomatoes, chickpeas and fish stock and bring to the boil. Reduce the heat and simmer uncovered for 15 minutes.

3 Add the fish and cook for 5 minutes or until the fish is just tender. Remove the soup from the heat, then add the couscous and cover. Set aside for 10 minutes or until the couscous is soft.

4 Serve with a dollop of yoghurt and sprinkled with parsley and mint.

SERVES 10

Moroccan Chickpea Lentil Soup

PREPARATION 30 mins **COOKING** 1 hr 10 mins

1 medium onion, sliced
2 stalks celery, chopped
3 cloves garlic, crushed
1 red capsicum, diced
2 teaspoons olive oil
½ teaspoon ground cinnamon
½ teaspoon ground ginger
½ teaspoon turmeric
6 cups vegetable stock
1⅓ cups lentils, rinsed
2 x 400g canned chickpeas, drained and rinsed
400g canned chopped tomatoes
¼ cup lemon juice
½ cup coriander, finely chopped
salt and freshly ground black pepper

1 Sauté onion, celery, garlic and capsicum in the oil until softened. Add cinnamon, ginger and turmeric.

2 Stirring thoroughly, add stock and lentils and bring to the boil. Reduce heat, cover and simmer for 45 minutes.

3 Add chickpeas and tomatoes and cook for another 15 minutes. Stir in lemon juice, coriander and salt and pepper to taste. Serve immediately.

SERVES 6

Chicken and Couscous Soup

PREPARATION 45 mins   COOKING 1 hr 15 mins

1½ kg chicken casserole pieces
400g canned diced tomatoes
1 onion, coarsely grated
½ teaspoon ground cumin
½ teaspoon paprika
½ teaspoon turmeric
⅛ teaspoon cayenne pepper or chilli powder
1 cinnamon stick
1 small clove garlic, crushed
salt and freshly ground black pepper
½ cup couscous
½ cup mint, chopped
¼ cup flat-leaf parsley, chopped
¼ cup coriander, chopped
2 teaspoons lemon juice

1 Place the chicken pieces in a large saucepan and add the tomatoes, onion, cumin, paprika, turmeric, cayenne or chilli, cinnamon, garlic, salt and pepper. Pour in 3 cups of water, bring to the boil, reduce heat, cover and simmer gently for 45–50 minutes until chicken is tender.

2 Remove the chicken with a slotted spoon to a plate. Cool, then remove the bones and discard. Cut chicken meat into small pieces and return to saucepan.

3 Add 5 more cups of water and bring back to a simmer. Slowly add the couscous, stirring constantly to distribute evenly. Add the mint, parsley and coriander. Simmer uncovered for 10 minutes, stirring occasionally. Add lemon juice, adjust seasoning if needed and serve immediately.

SERVES 6–8

Spicy Red Lentil and Pumpkin Soup

PREPARATION 15 mins **COOKING** 25 mins

375g red lentils
1 tablespoon olive oil
1 brown onion, finely chopped
2 cloves garlic, crushed
3 teaspoons ground cumin
2 teaspoons ground coriander
½ teaspoon chilli powder
½ teaspoon turmeric
1½ kg butternut pumpkin, peeled, deseeded, and cut into 1cm pieces
6½ cups vegetable stock
salt and freshly ground black pepper

1 Place the lentils in a sieve and rinse under cold running water.

2 Heat the oil in a large heavy-based saucepan over medium-high heat. Add the onion and cook, stirring often, for 5 minutes or until it softens. Add the garlic, cumin, coriander, chilli powder and turmeric. Cook, stirring, for 30 seconds or until aromatic.

3 Add the lentils and stir to coat in the onion mixture. Stir in the pumpkin and stock. Increase heat to high and bring to the boil. Reduce heat to medium-low and simmer, covered, stirring often, for 15 minutes or until pumpkin and lentils are very soft.

4 Taste and season with salt and pepper. Garnish with coriander or parsley sprigs to serve.

SERVES 4

Bessara

PREPARATION 30 mins **COOKING** 1 hr 5 mins

500g dried broad beans, soaked overnight
4 large cloves garlic
1 onion, diced
salt
½ cup virgin olive oil
2 teaspoons ground cumin
2 teaspoons paprika
¼ small bunch chives

1 Drain the soaked beans and remove the skins. Place in a large saucepan with enough water to cover, and the garlic and onion. Bring to the boil and boil at a steady pace for 40 minutes or until the beans are very soft – the time varies with different batches of beans. Skim off any froth as it rises to the surface, and add extra water if needed.

2 Place the beans, garlic, onion and some of the cooking water in a food processor and purée until smooth, adding extra liquid if needed.

3 Return the purée to a clean saucepan, place over low heat, stir in salt to taste, then the olive oil and spices and continue to cook until smooth and heated through. Add more cooking liquid to make a creamier consistency, if desired, and discard any unused cooking liquid.

4 Pour into individual soup bowls and garnish with extra paprika and a few chives diagonally across the surface. Serve with Moroccan Flat Bread, vegetable sticks and small jugs of olive oil and lemon juice.

SERVES 8

Harira

PREPARATION 40 mins   COOKING 2 hr 30 mins

500g lamb, cut into small cubes
1 teaspoon turmeric
1 teaspoon freshly ground black pepper
1 teaspoon ground cinnamon
¼ teaspoon ground ginger
30g butter
2 stalks celery and leaves, chopped
2 onions, chopped
¼ cup fresh parsley
¼ cup fresh coriander, chopped
800g canned chopped tomatoes
1 teaspoon salt
¾ cup lentils
1 cup canned chickpeas, drained and rinsed
¼ cup vermicelli
2 eggs
juice of ½ lemon

1 Put the lamb, spices, butter, celery, onion, parsley and coriander in a large saucepan and stir over a low heat for 5 minutes. Drain the tomatoes and reserve the juice, add the tomato flesh to the saucepan and continue cooking for 10–15 minutes. Salt lightly.

2 Add the juice from the tomatoes, 7 cups water and the lentils. Bring to the boil, then reduce heat, partially cover, and simmer for 2 hours.

3 When ready to serve, add the chickpeas and vermicelli and cook for 5 minutes. Beat the eggs with the lemon juice then, with the soup at a steady simmer, stir the lemony eggs into the stock with a long wooden spoon. Continue stirring slowly to create long egg strands and to thicken the soup. Season to taste, ladle into bowls and dust with cinnamon. Serve the extra lemon in a side bowl if desired.

SERVES 8–10

Vegetable Soup

PREPARATION 1 hr **COOKING** 1 hr

250g carrots, cut into small cubes
2 turnips, cut into small cubes
1 onion, finely sliced
5 small whole onions
1 leek, cut into slices
1 stalk celery, cut into small cubes
250g beef, cut into small cubes
3 small, fairly meaty mutton bones
1 teaspoon pepper
1 teaspoon salt
¼ teaspoon saffron
30g butter
250g potatoes
1kg tomatoes, chopped
4 sprigs coriander, chopped
60g vermicelli

1 Place carrots, turnips, onions, leek and celery in a saucepan with the meat and the bones. Season with the pepper, salt and saffron, add the butter and cover with fresh water.

2 Bring to the boil and leave to cook with the lid on for about 1 hour before adding the potatoes, tomatoes and coriander.

3 When the potatoes are cooked, gradually sprinkle in the vermicelli and simmer for a few minutes. Check the seasoning and serve.

SERVES 4

Moroccan Chickpea Soup

PREPARATION 30 mins COOKING 15 mins

2 tablespoons safflower oil
2 carrots, grated
2 cloves garlic, minced
1 onion, finely chopped
400g canned chickpeas, rinsed and drained
3 cups vegetable stock
⅓ cup tahini
2 tablespoons lemon juice
¼ cup fresh parsley, chopped
½ teaspoon thyme leaves
¾ tablespoon ground cumin
½ teaspoon freshly ground black pepper
¼ teaspoon turmeric
⅛ teaspoon cayenne pepper
1 tomato, diced
1 teaspoon toasted sesame seeds
1 green onion, finely chopped

1 In a 5-litre saucepan, heat the oil. Add carrots, garlic and onion and cook until tender. Set aside.

2 Meanwhile, in a food processor, purée chickpeas, 1 cup of vegetable stock, the tahini, and lemon juice.

3 Stir puréed mixture into saucepan. Add herbs and spices and remaining vegetable stock. Cover and cook for 5 minutes to heat through. Top with tomato, sesame seeds and green onion.

SERVES 4–6

Pea Soup

PREPARATION 30 mins **COOKING** 40 mins

500g yellow split peas
½ teaspoon salt
1 teaspoon ground cumin
6 cloves garlic, crushed

1 Pour 8 cups water into a pressure cooker and boil.

2 Wash dried peas and put them in pressure cooker. Add salt, cumin and garlic. Cover and cook for 30 minutes or until peas are completely cooked.

3 Remove from heat and allow to cool. In a food processor or blender, process until you get a thick soup.

4 Reheat soup and serve, sprinkled with cayenne pepper, paprika and olive oil and garnished with mint leaves.

Vegetables

Couscous is typically made with seven vegetables. To make couscous in the traditional way takes a lot of time and effort. However, if you buy it pre-packed, you can have steaming natural couscous in a matter of minutes.

Try combining the recipes in this chapter with couscous and you will have a complete meal in a very short time.

SERVES 4

Stewed Tomatoes with Okra and Coriander

PREPARATION 25 mins **COOKING** 35 mins

500g okra, trimmed and sliced
400g canned diced tomatoes
1 green capsicum, chopped
½ medium onion, finely chopped
1 bunch fresh coriander, chopped

1 Place sliced okra in a pan and cover with water. Bring to the boil and continue to cook for 5 minutes.

2 Drain, then add tomatoes, capsicum and onion. Simmer for 15–20 minutes, until okra is tender. Add 2 tablespoons coriander for final 2 minutes of cooking and season with salt, if desired. Serve garnished with remaining coriander.

SERVES 4–6

Moroccan Beans

PREPARATION 30 mins **COOKING** 20 mins

1 tablespoon vegetable oil
4cm piece fresh ginger, grated
1 teaspoon ground cinnamon
1 teaspoon cumin seeds
½ teaspoon turmeric
2 onions, chopped
400g canned red kidney beans, rinsed and drained
400g canned soy beans, rinsed and drained
400g canned chickpeas, rinsed and drained
400g tomato purée
1 cup vegetable stock
75g currants
60g pine nuts

1 Heat oil in a saucepan over a medium heat, add ginger, cinnamon, cumin seeds and turmeric and cook, stirring, for 1 minute. Add onions and cook for 3 minutes or until onions are soft.

2 Add kidney beans, soy beans, chickpeas, tomato paste and stock and bring to the boil. Reduce heat and simmer for 10 minutes.

3 Add currants and pine nuts and cook for 2 minutes longer before serving, garnished with coriander leaves.

SERVES 6

Moroccan Stuffed Artichokes

PREPARATION 40 mins COOKING 1 hr

2 tablespoons long-grain rice
6 large artichoke bottoms, uncooked
2 tablespoons olive oil
½ medium onion, finely chopped
125g lean minced beef
1 clove garlic, minced, plus 2 cloves sliced
¼ cup coriander, chopped
¼ teaspoon sweet paprika
¼ teaspoon ground cumin
⅛ teaspoon ground cinnamon
⅛ teaspoon ground ginger
¼ teaspoon salt
¼ teaspoon freshly ground pepper
4 Roma tomatoes, chopped
⅛ teaspoon turmeric

1 Boil rice uncovered in a small saucepan with 1 cup of boiling salted water for 10 minutes. Rinse with cold water and drain well. Transfer to a medium bowl.

2 Using a melon ball cutter, remove chokes and small purple leaves from centres of artichoke hearts. Rub with a cut lemon and put in a bowl of water.

3 Heat 1 tablespoon oil in a frying pan, add onion and cook over medium-low heat for 4–5 minutes. Add beef and sauté, stirring to crumble meat, for about 4 minutes or until meat changes colour. Remove from heat. Add minced garlic, coriander, paprika, cumin, cinnamon, ginger, salt and pepper and mix well. Add to rice and mix well again.

4 Sprinkle artichoke bottoms with additional salt and pepper. Spoon stuffing into artichoke bottoms. Pour remaining oil into a Dutch oven or wide casserole and add artichokes. Add tomatoes, sliced garlic, turmeric, a pinch of salt and pepper and 1 cup water. Bring to a simmer. Cover and cook over low heat for about 30 minutes or until artichokes are tender.

5 Serve hot, with a little tomato from the pan spooned over each artichoke.

SERVES 6–8

Spiced Caramelised Onions

PREPARATION 40 mins **COOKING** 50 mins

1 teaspoon ground ginger
1 teaspoon ground cinnamon
¼ teaspoon ground saffron
½ teaspoon turmeric
1 teaspoon coarsely ground black pepper
2 tablespoons olive oil
6 medium onions, peeled
2 tablespoons sugar

1 Preheat oven to 180°C. Mix together the four spices, black pepper and oil.

2 Slice the onions into 2cm slices. Brush slices each side with the spice mix and place in a greased shallow ovenproof pie plate or flan dish, 23cm in diameter, overlapping the slices. Pour over any remaining marinade and add 2 tablespoons water to the dish. Cover with foil, sealing the rim well.

3 Place on the centre shelf in the oven for 25 minutes – the onions will steam and soften. Remove foil, sprinkle with 1 tablespoon sugar and continue to cook uncovered for 20 minutes on top shelf until caramelised.

4 Heat remaining sugar in a small pan until it liquefies and turns amber in colour. Drizzle over surface of onions – it will set like toffee and give a nice crunch.

SERVES 4–6

Zucchini with Chermoula

PREPARATION 40 mins COOKING 1 hr 10 mins

1 kg zucchini

CHERMOULA

3 tablespoons olive oil
1 red onion, finely chopped
2 large cloves garlic, finely chopped
¼ teaspoon cayenne pepper
¼ teaspoon cracked black pepper
½ teaspoon paprika
½ teaspoon ground cumin
½ teaspoon salt
2 teaspoons preserved lemon, finely chopped
¼ cup fresh flat-leaf parsley, chopped
¼ cup fresh coriander, chopped

1 Trim ends off the zucchini. Cut in half lengthwise and cut each half into 3 or 4 sticks. Halve them again if too long.

2 Heat 2 tablespoons of the oil in a large saucepan, add the onion and fry for 3 minutes. Add the garlic and spices and stir for 30 seconds. Add the zucchini, salt, ⅓ cup water, the preserved lemon and the remaining oil if needed. Toss to coat with spices and cook over a medium heat for 15 minutes.

3 Add the parsley and coriander and continue to cook until zucchini is tender, about 10–15 minutes. Remove from heat and toss to mix. Transfer to a serving dish, garnish with extra preserved lemon strips and serve.

SERVES 4–6

Moroccan Pilaf

PREPARATION 10 mins **COOKING** 17 mins

1½ cups long-grain rice
1 tablespoon canola oil
4 green onions, sliced
1 tablespoon Moroccan seasoning
1 cup frozen peas, thawed
½ cup currants
⅓ cup slivered almonds, toasted

1 Cook the rice in a saucepan of boiling water for 10–12 minutes or until cooked. Drain and rinse.

2 Heat the oil in a wok over medium heat. Add the green onions and cook for 1–2 minutes. Add the Moroccan seasoning and stir to combine. Add the drained rice, peas, currants and slivered almonds. Stir-fry until heated through.

NOTE You can purchase toasted slivered almonds or you can toast them yourself. To toast the almonds, place them on a baking tray lined with baking paper and bake at 180°C for 4–5 minutes.

SERVES 4

Egg Capsicum Bhurji

PREPARATION 25 mins COOKING 20 mins

1 tablespoon olive oil
½ teaspoon cumin seeds
1 medium onion, finely chopped
¼ teaspoon turmeric
½ teaspoon chilli powder
salt
2 red capsicums, sliced
4 eggs

1 Heat the oil in a frying pan. Add cumin seeds and onion and fry until golden brown.

2 Add turmeric, chilli powder and salt to taste and stir well. Add capsicum, cover and simmer for 10 minutes.

3 Crack the eggs in and cook until done, about 5–7 minutes. Garnish with coriander or parsley leaves to serve.

SERVES 4

Moroccan Spiced Eggs and Tomatoes

PREPARATION 20 mins **COOKING** 30 mins

2 tablespoons olive oil
2 medium onions, finely chopped
4 cloves garlic, finely chopped
6 medium tomatoes, coarsely grated
4 eggs
¼ teaspoon salt
¼ teaspoon pepper
pinch of cayenne pepper
few drops of Tabasco

1 Preheat oven to 200°C. In a heavy-based frying pan, heat the olive oil. Sauté the onion and garlic until they begin to turn brown. Add the grated tomatoes, cover and cook over a low heat for 15 minutes.

2 Divide mixture into 4 ovenproof dishes. Break the eggs over the surface of each dishes and sprinkle with salt, pepper and cayenne to taste. Place into the oven and cook until the eggs are firm, about 5–7 minutes. Sprinkle with Tabasco and serve hot, garnished with coriander leaves.

SERVES 4

Hot and Spicy Vegetable Tagine with Chickpeas

PREPARATION 45 mins **COOKING** 1 hr 15 mins

½ cup dried chickpeas, soaked in cold water overnight
2 tablespoons vegetable oil
1 large onion, thinly sliced
1 large fresh red chilli, deseeded and chopped
1 red capsicum, chopped
4 cloves garlic, chopped
2 carrots, chopped
300g sweet potato, peeled and chopped
4 tomatoes, chopped
300g potatoes, peeled and chopped
1 stalk celery, sliced
200g green beans, halved

SPICE MIX

1 tablespoon cumin seeds, roasted
1 tablespoon coriander seeds, roasted
2 teaspoons sweet paprika
1 teaspoon salt
½ teaspoon cayenne pepper
½ teaspoon freshly ground black pepper

YOGHURT DRESSING

½ cup natural yoghurt
1 tablespoon lemon juice
1 clove garlic, crushed
2 sprigs fresh dill, finely chopped
2 sprigs fresh mint, finely chopped
grated zest of ½ lemon

1 To make spice mix, combine all spices and grind in a food processor or blender until very fine.

2 To make yoghurt dressing, mix yoghurt, lemon juice, garlic, herbs and lemon zest. Set aside.

3 Cook drained chickpeas in simmering water, uncovered, for about 30 minutes or until tender. Drain.

4 Heat oil in a large tagine and cook onion, chilli, capsicum and 2 tablespoons of the spice mix over low heat until onion is soft, adding a little water if onion is sticking to the tagine. Reserve any remaining spice mix for later use.

5 Add chickpeas, garlic, remaining vegetables and 1 cup water and season to taste. Cook, covered, over low heat for about 30 minutes or until vegetables are tender. Serve drizzled with yoghurt dressing.

SERVES 4

Moroccan Saffron Rice

PREPARATION 25 mins **COOKING** 30 mins

2 tablespoons vegetable oil
1 medium onion, chopped
1 green capsicum, chopped
1 cup long-grain rice
½ teaspoon salt
¼ teaspoon black pepper
¼ teaspoon saffron

1 Heat oil in a large frying pan. Stir in the onion, capsicum and rice. Fry over moderate heat, stirring frequently, until the rice becomes golden, about 5 minutes.

2 Add salt, pepper, saffron and 2 cups water and bring to the boil. Reduce heat and simmer for about 20 minutes until liquid is absorbed. Sprinkle with pistachio nuts to serve.

Seafood

While the importance of seafood is increasing in the Moroccan diet, barbecued seafood has long been very popular on the streets and in the homes of the Moroccan people. Fish and shellfish are plentiful due to the long coastline.

We have developed a great series of recipes for a wide range of seafood in this chapter – try and enjoy!

SERVES 4

Sardines with Coriander and Lime

PREPARATION 35 mins **COOKING** 10 mins

8 small sardines, cleaned and gutted
½ teaspoon salt
2 limes
1 green chilli, thinly sliced
1 cup fresh coriander, chopped
1 tablespoon olive oil

1 Season the insides of the fish with salt, then make 2–3 shallow diagonal cuts on both sides of each fish.

2 Grate the zest and squeeze the juice from 1 lime, and slice the other lime thinly. In a small bowl, mix together the lime juice, zest and sliced chilli, then rub this mixture into the fish, both inside and out. Place the fish in a shallow dish, then scatter the coriander over the top and cover with the slices of lime. Refrigerate for 1 hour.

3 Remove the fish from the dish and brush liberally with olive oil. Place in an oiled hinged wire fish grill and barbecue the oiled side over medium coals for 3–4 minutes.

4 Brush the other side of the fish with oil, turn and continue to cook for a further 3–4 minutes. Serve immediately.

SERVES 8

Curried Seafood Stew

PREPARATION 1 hr **COOKING** 50 mins

500g white fish, cut into chunks
500g scallops
8 cups chicken stock
1 large onion, roughly diced
1 small fennel bulb, diced
2 jalapeños, sliced
2 carrots, diced
2 potatoes, diced
1 small red capsicum, diced
2 tablespoons curry powder, toasted
zest of 2 lemons
2 tablespoons lemon juice
2 tablespoons ground cumin, toasted
¼ cup olives, chopped
250g canned chickpeas, drained and rinsed
1 eggplant, roasted and diced
¼ cup parsley, coarsely chopped
¼ cup coriander, coarsely chopped
500g prawns, peeled, tails left intact

1 Sear the fish and scallops until golden brown – don't overcook – then set aside.

2 Bring the chicken stock to the boil and add the onion, fennel, jalapeños, carrots, and potatoes. Cook for 20 minutes.

3 Add the rest of the ingredients except the seafood. Cook until all the vegetables are tender.

4 Add all the seafood and cook until prawns are done. Adjust seasoning to taste and serve.

MAKES 20

Seafood Rolls

PREPARATION 45 mins COOKING 40 mins

125g crab meat
200g medium raw prawns
1½ tablespoons olive oil
1 small onion, finely chopped
2 cloves garlic, crushed
½ teaspoon ground cumin
½ teaspoon paprika
¼ teaspoon ground saffron
pinch of cayenne pepper
1 large tomato, skinned, deseeded and diced
¼ cup fresh coriander, finely chopped
¼ cup fresh breadcrumbs
375g filo pastry
olive oil

1 Preheat oven to 180°C. Flake the crab meat and remove any sinew. Shell the prawns and cut into small pieces.

2 Heat oil in a frying pan, sauté the onion and garlic for 1 minute, add the spices and stir quickly until aromatic. Stir in the diced tomato, cook a little, then add the chopped prawns and cook until they just turn pink. Mix in the coriander and breadcrumbs to combine well. Remove from heat and set aside.

3 Cut 1 sheet of filo into 3 equal strips, then repeat with another sheet. Lightly spray or brush 2 strips with oil and put one on top of the other, making a double layer of filo. Do the same with the other 4 strips of filo, making 3 strips of double-layered filo.

4 Place a tablespoonful of mixture on each strip 2cm in from the end and sides. Lift end piece over filling. Turn in the side strips all the way up, brush sides and top end lightly with water and roll to the end. Place seam-side down on a greased oven tray and spray or brush lightly with oil. Repeat this process until all the filo and filling is used.

5 Bake for 20–25 minutes until golden and crisp. Serve hot.

SERVES 4

Pan-Seared Moroccan-Style Tuna

PREPARATION 25 mins **COOKING** 10 mins

4 tuna steaks, about 25mm thick and 150g each
1 teaspoon paprika
½ teaspoon ground cumin
1 teaspoon turmeric
¼ teaspoon ground anise seed
½ teaspoon ground ginger
⅛ teaspoon ground cinnamon
¼ teaspoon red pepper flakes
salt and freshly ground black pepper
1 tablespoon freshly squeezed lemon juice
2 tablespoons extra virgin olive oil
30g butter, melted
½ cup fresh coriander, chopped

1 Rinse the tuna steaks and pat dry with absorbent paper.

2 In a small bowl, combine paprika, cumin, turmeric, anise, ginger, cinnamon, pepper flakes, salt, pepper and lemon juice. Lightly rub both sides of the tuna steaks with olive oil. Rub the seasoning mix on both sides of tuna steaks, coating them well.

3 Using a heavy-bottomed frying pan, warm the remaining olive oil. Increase the heat to high and place the tuna in the pan. Sear for 1 minute, then turn over carefully, reducing the heat to medium. Sear the other side for about 1 minute until medium rare – do not overcook tuna or the meat will become dry and lose its flavour.

4 Pour the melted butter over the tuna steaks directly after you take them from the pan, then sprinkle with coriander. Serve immediately with couscous.

SERVES 4

Fish Tagine with Raisins and Honey

PREPARATION 35 mins **COOKING** 30 mins

3 tablespoons olive oil
¼ teaspoon ground cumin
¼ teaspoon cayenne pepper
¼ teaspoon ground saffron
½ teaspoon ground cinnamon
4 fish cutlets
1 large red onion, finely diced
¼ teaspoon freshly ground black pepper
4 tablespoons honey
4 tablespoons wine vinegar
¾ cup raisins, soaked and drained
¼ cup flat-leaf parsley, finely chopped

1 Combine 1 tablespoon olive oil with the cumin, cayenne, saffron and ¼ teaspoon cinnamon and rub into the fish cutlets on both sides. Place on plate, cover and refrigerate for 2 hours to allow flavours to penetrate.

2 Heat remaining oil in a tagine and sear the fish on both sides until lightly coloured. Remove immediately and set aside.

3 Add the diced onion to the tagine, adding extra oil if needed, and fry gently while stirring until soft. Stir in pepper, remaining cinnamon, honey, vinegar, raisins and parsley. Turn heat to low and simmer for 10 minutes. Return the fish to the tagine, spoon some sauce over the fish, cover and simmer for 10 minutes, basting occasionally with sauce. Serve immediately with rice or couscous.

SERVES 4

Moroccan Fish with Fresh Tomato Sauce

PREPARATION 2 hrs 45 mins **COOKING** 15 mins

750g white fish fillets, skinned
1 medium red onion, finely chopped
1 clove garlic, crushed
¼ cup fresh coriander, chopped
⅓ cup fresh flat-leaf parsley, chopped
½ teaspoon ground sweet paprika
¼ teaspoon chilli powder
⅓ cup olive oil
2 tablespoons lemon juice

TOMATO SAUCE

4 large tomatoes, peeled, deseeded and chopped
2 small red chillies, deseeded and finely sliced
4 green onions, finely sliced
½ bunch fresh coriander, finely chopped
½ cup olive oil
freshly ground black pepper
1 teaspoon lime juice
1 red onion, finely chopped

1 Cut fish across grain into 2cm cubes. Combine onion, garlic, coriander, parsley, paprika, chilli powder, olive oil and lemon juice and spoon over fish. Mix well and leave to marinate for at least 2 hours or overnight.

2 Place fish on metal skewers and grill, turning frequently, until lightly browned on all sides.

3 To make tomato sauce, combine tomatoes, chillies, green onions and coriander in a bowl, then add olive oil and pepper to taste. Add lime juice and red onion. Refrigerate the tomato sauce for at least 1 hour before serving with fish.

SERVES 4

Marinated Fish Skewers with Chermoula

PREPARATION 1 hr 35 mins **COOKING** 15 mins

750g thick white fish steaks
1 small onion
1 clove garlic, crushed
1 teaspoon paprika
½ teaspoon ground cumin
3 tablespoons olive oil
2 tablespoons lemon juice
½ teaspoon salt

CHERMOULA

½ teaspoon ground coriander
2 teaspoons ground cumin
1 teaspoon paprika
3 cloves garlic, crushed
⅓ cup olive oil
¼ cup lemon juice
½ cup fresh coriander, chopped
1 small red onion, finely chopped

1 Cut the fish into 2cm cubes and place into a large non-metallic dish. Grate the onion into a bowl, add the garlic, spices, oil, lemon juice and salt. Mix well and pour over the fish, turning to coat all sides. Cover and marinate 1 hour or more in the refrigerator. Meanwhile, soak 8 bamboo skewers in water.

2 To make the chermoula, heat the spices in a small pan for about 30 seconds until fragrant. Combine with the garlic, oil and lemon juice and whisk well until thick. Stir in the coriander and onion. Set aside.

3 Thread the fish cubes onto the skewers. Grill under a hot grill or on an oiled grill plate or barbecue. Serve on a bed of saffron rice with the chermoula drizzled over the fish.

SERVES 4

Fish Tagine with Currants

PREPARATION 15 mins **COOKING** 1 hr

1 tablespoon olive oil
1 red onion, halved and cut into thin wedges
2 cloves garlic, crushed
1 teaspoon ground cinnamon
400g canned chopped tomatoes
500g firm white fish fillets, cut into 25mm pieces
1 large zucchini, trimmed, halved lengthwise and thinly sliced diagonally
150g green beans, cut into 25mm lengths
½ teaspoon freshly ground black pepper
1 cup couscous
1 tablespoon currants
¼ cup fresh flat-leaf parsley, chopped

1 Preheat oven to 180°C. Heat the oil in a large non-stick frying pan over medium heat. Add the onion and cook, stirring occasionally, for 5 minutes or until soft. Add the garlic and cinnamon and cook, stirring, for about 1 minute.

2 Add the tomatoes and ½ cup water and stir until well combined. Increase heat to high and bring to the boil, then reduce heat to medium. Simmer for 5 minutes.

3 Cover the base of a tagine with some of the sauce. Add the fish and pour remainder of the sauce over with the zucchini and beans. Simmer for 3 minutes to start the cooking process. Season with pepper, then transfer the tagine to the oven and cook for 40–45 minutes.

4 Place the couscous in a large heatproof bowl. Add 1 cup boiling water. Cover and set aside for 3 minutes or until the liquid is absorbed. Use a fork to separate the grains.

5 Divide the couscous among serving dishes, then top with the fish mixture. Sprinkle with the currants and parsley to serve.

SERVES 4

Piquant Prawns

PREPARATION 25 mins COOKING 10 mins

½ cup olive oil
6 cloves garlic, minced
3 tablespoons red wine vinegar
400g canned diced tomatoes
1 teaspoon red chilli flakes
500g large prawns, shelled and deveined
½ cup fresh basil, chopped
½ cup fresh flat-leaf parsley, chopped
salt and freshly ground black pepper

1 Gently warm olive oil in a large frying pan. Add garlic and cook for a few minutes. Add vinegar and tomatoes, continue to cook over low heat. Stir in the chilli flakes. Add prawns and simmer until just cooked through, turning often, about 5 minutes.

2 Remove from heat. Add basil, parsley, salt and pepper. Garnish with a few extra parsley sprigs and serve.

Poultry

Poultry was historically the most important meat used in Morocco. In fact, today Morocco still has a large export market for fresh poultry. Many offerings in this chapter feature traditional cooking methods passed down through the generations – we're sure you will be pleased with the results of these time-honoured recipes.

SERVES 4

Chicken Casablanca

PREPARATION 30 mins **COOKING** 6 hrs

2 onions, sliced
1cm piece fresh ginger, grated
3 cloves garlic, minced
2 tablespoons olive oil
1½ kg skinless chicken pieces
3 carrots, diced
2 potatoes, peeled and diced
3 zucchini, cut into 25mm slices
3 dry apricots
3 prunes
½ teaspoon ground cumin
½ teaspoon turmeric
½ teaspoon salt
½ teaspoon black pepper
¼ teaspoon ground cinnamon
¼ teaspoon cayenne pepper
2 tablespoons seedless raisins
400g canned chopped tomatoes
400g canned chickpeas, drained and rinsed
¼ cup flat-leaf parsley, chopped
½ teaspoon ground coriander

1 In a large frying pan, sauté onions, ginger and garlic in oil. Transfer to slow cooker. In the same frying pan, brown chicken over medium heat.

2 Add carrots, potatoes, zucchini, dry apricots and prunes to slow cooker. Place browned chicken on top of vegetables. Stir seasonings in a small bowl and sprinkle over chicken. Add raisins and tomatoes.

3 Cover and cook on high for 4–6 hours.
Add chickpeas, parsley and coriander 30 minutes before serving. Serve over rice or couscous.

SERVES 4

Chicken Tagine with Couscous

PREPARATION 25 mins COOKING 25 mins

2 tablespoons olive oil
4 chicken thigh fillets, about 180g each, halved
1 brown onion, halved and thinly sliced
2 cloves garlic, crushed
1 tablespoon Moroccan spice mix
400g canned diced tomatoes
400g canned chickpeas, drained and rinsed
1 zucchini, halved and cut into 25mm pieces
salt and freshly ground black pepper
½ cup couscous
¼ cup fresh coriander

1 Heat 1 tablespoon of oil in a large tagine over high heat. Add chicken and cook for 2 minutes each side or until light golden. Remove to a plate.

2 Reduce heat to medium. Add onion and garlic. Cook, stirring occasionally, for 2–3 minutes or until onion is tender. Add spice mix and cook for 30 seconds or until aromatic.

3 Return chicken to tagine. Add tomatoes, chickpeas and zucchini. Bring to the boil, reduce heat to low, then cover and simmer, stirring occasionally, for 12–15 minutes or until chicken is tender and cooked through. Season with salt and pepper.

4 Meanwhile, place ½ cups cold water in a medium saucepan. Bring to the boil over high heat. Remove saucepan from heat and stir in couscous. Cover and stand for 10 minutes or until liquid is absorbed. Fluff couscous with a fork to separate grains.

5 Spoon couscous onto plates. Spoon over chicken tagine, sprinkle with coriander and serve immediately.

SERVES 6

Moroccan Chicken with Chickpeas

PREPARATION 35 mins **COOKING** 1 hr

3 tablespoons olive oil
1½ kg chicken pieces
1 large red onion, thinly sliced
1 teaspoon turmeric
¼ teaspoon paprika
½ teaspoon salt
4 cups chicken stock
400g canned chickpeas, drained and rinsed
juice of 1 lemon
freshly ground black pepper
¼ cup flat-leaf parsley, chopped
¼ cup coriander, chopped

1 Heat the oil in a large saucepan or frying pan and brown the chicken pieces a few at a time. Remove to a plate. Add the onion and cook gently until soft and slightly golden. Drain some of the oil from the pan if you wish.

2 Add spices and stir for a few seconds. Return chicken pieces to the pan and turn to coat well with the spices. Add the chicken stock, chickpeas, lemon juice and pepper. Bring to the boil, then reduce heat and simmer covered for 40 minutes.

3 Add the parsley and coriander and simmer 10–15 minutes more until chicken is very tender and sauce is reduced.

4 Remove to a serving dish or platter, sprinkle lightly with extra chopped parsley and serve with Moroccan Flat Bread.

SERVES 4–6

Spiced Chicken Drumsticks

PREPARATION 1 hr **COOKING** 1 hr 30 mins

2 cloves garlic, crushed
¼ teaspoon ground saffron
¼ teaspoon ground cumin
¼ teaspoon paprika
pinch of cayenne pepper
½ teaspoon salt
freshly ground black pepper
2 tablespoons lemon juice
12 chicken drumsticks
2 tablespoons olive oil
30g butter
¼ cup plain flour
1 onion, finely sliced
8 preserved lemon segments
1½ teaspoons chicken stock powder
3 large ripe tomatoes, skinned, halved and deseeded
¼ cup coriander, finely chopped
10 black olives
¼ cup parsley, finely chopped

1 Mix the garlic, spices, seasonings and lemon juice together. Rub the drumsticks well with the mixture using your fingers, place in a non-metallic container and marinate for 2 hours or longer in the refrigerator.

2 Heat oil and butter in a wide-based saucepan or frying pan. Dust each drumstick with flour. Place in the pan a few at a time and turn to brown on all sides. Add the onion, preserved lemon, stock powder and enough water to just cover the chicken, about 2–2½ cups.

3 Place the tomato halves over the chicken and sprinkle in the coriander. Bring to the boil then turn down and simmer for 1 hour. After 40 minutes, add the olives.

4 Lift drumsticks onto a heated serving platter, cover and keep hot. Place any large pieces of cooked tomato on top then boil the remaining sauce, uncovered, to reduce down until thickened. Pour the sauce over the chicken. Sprinkle with finely chopped parsley and serve immediately with Moroccan Flat Bread.

SERVES 4

Moroccan Chicken and Vegetable Rolls

PREPARATION 25 mins **COOKING** 25 mins

2 tablespoons olive oil
1 medium brown onion, finely diced
500g chicken mince
3 teaspoons Moroccan spice mix
1 medium carrot, grated
1 medium zucchini, grated
2 egg yolks
salt and freshly ground black pepper
2 sheets puff pastry, thawed
1 tablespoon milk
1½ tablespoons sesame seeds

1 Preheat oven to 200°C and line an oven tray with baking paper. Heat oil in a small frying pan over a medium-high heat. Add the onion and cook for 3 minutes, stirring often, until soft. Remove and set aside. Combine chicken, Moroccan spice, carrot, zucchini and egg yolks in a bowl. Add the onion and season with salt and pepper. Mix thoroughly.

2 Cut each pastry sheet in half. Divide chicken mixture evenly between the 4 pieces of pastry, forming a long, thick sausage down the middle of each piece. Brush one edge of each piece of pastry with milk and fold the pastry over to totally enclose the filling. Trim ends of any excess pastry, then cut each roll in half.

3 Place the rolls on the prepared oven tray and brush with milk. Slash the top of each with a knife in a few places to expose the filling, then sprinkle with sesame seeds. Bake for 20–25 minutes or until the pastry is golden brown.

4 Serve with a bowl of steamed baby carrots and pumpkin, scattered with toasted slivered almonds and drizzled with olive oil.

SERVES 4

Chicken in Almond Sauce

PREPARATION 45 mins **COOKING** 45 mins

¾ cup sliced almonds
1kg chicken drumsticks
1 teaspoon salt
1 cinnamon stick
1 teaspoon dried oregano
2 bay leaves
2 tablespoons vegetable oil
3 rindless rashers bacon, chopped
1 onion, chopped
4 cloves garlic, chopped
1 cup chicken stock
½ teaspoon freshly ground black pepper
¼ cup flat-leaf parsley, chopped

1 Put oven rack in middle position and preheat oven to 190°C.

2 Spread ¼ cup almonds on a baking sheet and toast in oven until golden, about 8–10 minutes.

3 Finely grind remaining ½ cup almonds in a food processor for about 1 minute (don't grind to a paste). Pat chicken dry with absorbent paper and sprinkle with ½ teaspoon salt.

4 Heat a dry 30cm heavy-based frying pan over moderate heat, then toast ground almonds, cinnamon stick, oregano and bay leaves, stirring constantly, until almonds are pale golden, about 2 minutes. Transfer to a bowl and wipe frying pan clean.

5 Heat oil in frying pan over high heat until hot but not smoking, then sauté chicken, turning over once, until golden, about 5 minutes total. Transfer chicken to a plate.

6 Add bacon to frying pan and cook over moderate heat, stirring, until bacon begins to render fat and turn golden, about 1 minute. Add onion and garlic and cook, stirring occasionally, until golden, about 3 minutes. Stir in ground almond mixture and chicken stock and boil for 1 minute, scraping up brown bits from the pan. Stir in pepper and remaining ½ teaspoon salt.

7 Add chicken, turning to coat, then reduce heat to moderate and simmer, covered, until chicken is just cooked through, about 5 minutes. Stir in parsley and sliced almonds. Discard cinnamon stick and bay leaves. Serve chicken with sauce spooned on top.

SERVES 4

Moroccan Chicken Stir-Fry

PREPARATION 30 mins COOKING 30 mins

1 tablespoon olive oil
2 chicken breasts, chopped
1 onion, finely chopped
100g fresh green beans, coarsely chopped
2 large cloves garlic, minced
3cm piece ginger, minced
1 teaspoon paprika
zest of ½ lemon
2 teaspoons ground cumin
1 teaspoon turmeric
½ teaspoon cayenne pepper
1 tablespoon dried oregano
400g canned chopped tomatoes
1 cup chicken stock
400g canned chickpeas, drained and rinsed
1 cup couscous
15 dried apricots, finely chopped

1 Heat oil in saucepan and brown chicken, then remove from pan. Add to the pan the onion, beans, garlic, ginger, paprika, lemon zest, cumin, turmeric, cayenne and oregano and stir-fry for 1 minute. Return chicken to pan, add tomatoes and chicken stock, simmer for 15 minutes. Add drained chickpeas, simmer for further 5 minutes.

2 Place the couscous in a large heatproof bowl and add 1 cups boiling water. Cover and set aside until the liquid is absorbed, about 15 minutes. Fluff with a fork and stir through apricots. Serve chicken with couscous and a wedge of lemon.

SERVES 4

Moroccan Chicken with Couscous

PREPARATION 15 mins **COOKING** 55 mins

50g pine nuts
¼ cup plain flour, seasoned with salt and pepper
500g skinless chicken thigh fillets, cut into 25mm dice
4 tablespoons olive oil
2 onions, sliced
1 teaspoon ground cinnamon
1 teaspoon ground cumin
1 teaspoon mild paprika
1 teaspoon ground coriander
1 teaspoon sultanas
3 cups chicken stock
2 cups couscous
¼ cup fresh coriander, chopped
juice of 1 lemon
1 cup natural yoghurt

1 Heat a large non-stick frying pan over medium-high heat. Add pine nuts, stirring constantly, until just starting to colour. Transfer pine nuts to a plate.

2 Place seasoned flour in a large bowl, add chicken and toss to coat. Add one tablespoon of oil to the frying pan, increase heat to high and cook half the chicken until golden. Transfer cooked chicken to a plate. Repeat with another tablespoon of oil and remaining chicken.

3 Heat another tablespoon of oil in frying pan. Add onions, reduce heat to medium and cook, stirring frequently, for 10 minutes or until golden and softened. Add cooked chicken to frying pan with spices, sultanas and 1 cup of stock.

4 Bring to the boil, then reduce heat to low and cook for 5–10 minutes until heated through and thickened.

5 Meanwhile, bring remaining chicken stock to the boil in a small saucepan, stir in couscous and final tablespoon of olive oil and turn off heat. Leave for 5 minutes, then use a fork to separate the couscous grains.

6 Just before serving, stir the pine nuts, coriander and lemon juice through the chicken. Serve with the couscous and yoghurt.

SERVES 4

Moroccan Chicken, Lemon and Olives

PREPARATION 30 mins **COOKING** 20 mins

1 tablespoon olive oil
1 white onion, finely chopped
2 cloves garlic, crushed
1 chicken breast fillet, diced
1 teaspoon ground cumin
1 teaspoon ground turmeric
1 teaspoon ground ginger
1 teaspoon ground fennel
¼ cup chicken stock
1 tomato, diced
⅓ cup black olives
1 preserved lemon wedge, pulp removed, zest thinly sliced
¼ cup fresh coriander, chopped
¼ cup fresh flat-leaf parsley, chopped
¼ bunch chives, chopped

1 Heat oil in a frying pan over medium heat, cook onion and garlic for 2 minutes, add the chicken and spices and cook for 4–5 minutes, stirring occasionally to brown the chicken all over.

2 Add stock, tomato, olives and lemon to the frying pan, simmer for 4–5 minutes or until chicken is cooked through. Stir through the herbs just before serving.

Meat

Every part of the country has its regional tagine dish and different ways of preparing it. Tagines of meat are typically served with couscous and often a salad.

Beef is the most commonly eaten red meat in Morocco. Lamb is preferred, but is not as common due to its higher cost. The breed of sheep in North Africa has much of its fat concentrated in its tail, which means that Moroccan lamb does not have the pungent flavour that Western lamb and mutton can have.

SERVES 4

Moroccan Lamb Pizza

PREPARATION 40 mins **COOKING** 25 mins

1 tablespoon sunflower oil
1 red onion, finely chopped
1 clove garlic, crushed
250g lean minced lamb
½ cup canned crushed tomatoes
1 teaspoon ground cumin
1 teaspoon ground coriander
½ teaspoon ground cinnamon
¼ cup fresh coriander, chopped
1 tablespoon lemon juice
4 single-serve pizza bases
1 tablespoon pine nuts, toasted
125g mozzarella cheese, torn
1 cup fresh mint leaves
1 cup fresh flat-leaf parsley
freshly ground black pepper
2 tablespoons mango relish

RAITA

½ cup natural yoghurt
1 Lebanese cucumber, grated
1 clove garlic, crushed
¼ cup fresh mint, chopped

1 Heat the oil in a frying pan, add the onion and garlic and cook over a medium heat for 1 minute. Add the lamb and cook until browned, breaking the meat up with a fork. Drain any excess oil from the pan. Add the tomatoes, cumin, ground coriander and cinnamon and cook for 5 minutes. Stir in the fresh coriander and half the lemon juice.

2 Preheat the oven to 200°C. Spread the lamb topping over the pizza bases and sprinkle with the pine nuts and mozzarella. Bake for 10 minutes or until the cheese has melted and the pizzas are heated through.

3 To make the raita, mix the yoghurt, cucumber, garlic and mint in a bowl.

4 Toss the mint and parsley leaves in the remaining lemon juice and season with pepper. Serve the pizzas topped with the herb leaves, raita and mango relish.

SERVES 4–6

Lamb and Chickpea Tagine

PREPARATION 20 mins **COOKING** 2 hrs 20 mins

3 tablespoons olive oil
1kg lamb leg, diced into 2cm pieces
salt and freshly ground black pepper
2 onions, diced
2 cloves garlic, finely chopped
2 teaspoons ground cumin
1 teaspoon ground coriander
1 teaspoon turmeric
½ teaspoon ground ginger
2 teaspoons paprika
¼ teaspoon cayenne pepper
pinch of saffron threads
1 cup chicken stock
2 large potatoes, peeled and diced
400g canned diced tomatoes
1 cup canned chickpeas, drained and rinsed
100g dried apricots

1 Place the tagine base on a medium heat. When hot, add the oil and lamb, seal all over and season with salt and pepper. Add the onions and garlic and fry until translucent. Add all the spices and cook, stirring, for 5 minutes. Add the stock, potatoes, tomatoes and chickpeas and stir thoroughly.

2 Cover the tagine and reduce to a low heat. Simmer for 1½–2 hours, until the meat is tender, then remove the lid and add the apricots. Continue cooking for a few more minutes to thicken the sauce. Serve at the table, in the tagine.

SERVES 4–6

Moroccan Spiced Pork

PREPARATION 30 mins **COOKING** 15 mins

2½ teaspoons ground coriander
1½ teaspoons ground cumin
1 teaspoon sweet paprika
1 teaspoon chilli paste
500g lean pork stir-fry strips
2½ tablespoons vegetable oil
2 cloves garlic, sliced
15mm piece fresh ginger, grated
250g pumpkin, sliced
100g baby English spinach
¼ cup fresh coriander, chopped
1 tablespoon fresh lemon juice

1 Combine ground coriander, cumin, paprika and chilli paste and rub into pork.

2 Use 2 tablespoons of the oil to cook pork. Heat 1 tablespoon oil in a large wok over medium-high heat, add half the pork and stir-fry for 1–2 minutes, stirring continuously. Transfer to a plate, cover loosely with foil and set aside. Repeat with another tablespoon of oil and remaining pork.

3 Reduce heat to medium, add remaining ½ tablespoon oil and cook garlic for 2 minutes. Add ginger and pumpkin and cook for 3 minutes, stirring continuously.

4 Return pork to wok, add spinach, fresh coriander and lemon juice. Stir to combine and cook for 2 minutes to heat pork through. Serve immediately with couscous.

MAKES 20

Spicy Lamb Triangles

PREPARATION 20 mins   COOKING 30 mins

1 tablespoon olive oil
1 small brown onion, halved and finely chopped
1 clove garlic, crushed
1½ tablespoons Moroccan spice mix
250g lamb mince
45g dried dates, finely chopped
45g slivered almonds, toasted
¼ cup natural yoghurt
¼ cup fresh coriander, coarsely chopped
salt and freshly ground black pepper
20 sheets filo pastry
60g butter, melted

1 Heat the oil in a large frying pan over medium-high heat. Add the onion and garlic and cook, stirring, for 5 minutes or until onion softens. Add the spice mix and cook, stirring, for 2 minutes or until fragrant.

2 Add the lamb and cook, stirring with a wooden spoon to break up any lumps, for 5 minutes or until golden brown. Remove from heat. Add the dates, almonds, yoghurt and coriander, and stir to combine. Taste and season with salt and pepper. Set aside for 15 minutes to cool.

3 Place the filo sheets on a clean work bench. Cover with a clean tea towel, then a damp tea towel (this will prevent it drying out). Brush 1 filo sheet with melted butter and fold lengthwise into 3 to make a 5cm-wide strip of pastry. Place 1 tablespoon of the mince mixture on the narrow edge closest to you. Use your fingers to hold the mince in place and fold the bottom right-hand corner over diagonally to cover filling. Fold on the straight, then on the diagonal, and keep folding in this manner until the end of the pastry strip is reached and a triangle forms. Place on a baking tray. Repeat with the remaining pastry, melted butter and filling.

4 Preheat oven to 180°C. Brush triangles with any remaining melted butter. Bake for 15 minutes or until heated through and golden brown. Remove from oven. Arrange triangles on a large serving platter and serve immediately.

SERVES 8

Berber-Style Lamb

PREPARATION 45 mins **COOKING** 2 hrs

- 1 cup fresh coriander, very coarsely chopped
- 1 cup fresh mint leaves
- 1 cup olive oil
- 12cm piece fresh ginger, chopped
- 8 large cloves garlic, peeled
- 1 tablespoon ground cumin
- 2 teaspoons freshly ground black pepper
- 2 teaspoons cardamom seeds
- 1½ teaspoons allspice
- 1¼ teaspoons salt
- 1½ teaspoons turmeric
- 1 teaspoon ground coriander
- 3 large red capsicums, quartered lengthwise
- 2 red onions, cut into 6 wedges each
- 2 large sweet potatoes, peeled and cut diagonally into 25mm-thick rounds
- 3kg semi-boneless leg of lamb, tied to hold its shape
- 3½ cups chicken stock
- 1½ cups couscous

1 Purée first 12 ingredients in food processor. Toss capsicums, onions and sweet potato in a large roasting pan with ½ cup of the spice purée.

2 Place lamb fat-side down in centre of pan. Rub ½ cup spice purée inside lamb, then make sure you rub spices all over outside of lamb. Turn lamb fat-side up. Cover and refrigerate lamb and remaining spice purée overnight.

3 Position rack in lower third of oven and preheat to 230°C. Roast lamb for 25 minutes. Reduce oven temperature to 180°C. Roast for about 1 hour 10 minutes.

4 Transfer lamb to a platter. Spoon vegetables around lamb. Tent with foil to keep warm. Place roasting pan over 2 burners on stove top at high heat, add 2 cups stock and bring to the boil, scraping up browned bits. Boil until reduced to 1½ cups, about 8 minutes. Pour gravy into sauceboat. Spoon fat off surface and discard. Whisk 2 tablespoons spice purée into gravy and set aside.

5 Place same roasting pan over high heat. Add remaining stock and 1 tablespoon spice purée and bring to the boil. Mix in couscous. Remove from heat and cover tightly with foil. Let stand until liquid is absorbed, about 8 minutes. Fluff couscous with a fork. Spoon couscous in pockets around lamb and vegetables on platter. Serve with gravy.

SERVES 4–6

Meatball Stew

PREPARATION 40 mins **COOKING** 50 mins

MEATBALLS

500g lamb mince
¼ cup fresh parsley, chopped
¼ cup fresh coriander, chopped
½ teaspoon ground cumin
½ onion, finely chopped
¼ teaspoon cayenne pepper
salt
2 tablespoons olive oil

STEW

2 cloves garlic, peeled
2 medium onions, finely chopped
1 green capsicum, chopped
1 small bunch parsley, chopped
1kg tomatoes, chopped
1 teaspoon ground cumin
1 teaspoon freshly ground black pepper
½ teaspoon ground cinnamon
2 tablespoons fresh lemon juice
¼ teaspoon cayenne pepper
1½ teaspoons salt
6 eggs

1 Combine all the ingredients for the meatballs except the oil and form into 25mm balls with wet hands. Heat a large, heavy-based saucepan or casserole dish and add the olive oil. Brown the meatballs in the oil, then remove, leaving the oil in the pan. Set the meatballs aside, covered.

2 Add the garlic, onion, and capsicum to the reserved oil and sauté until the onion is clear. Add the remaining sauce ingredients except the eggs and simmer, covered, for 30 minutes until the sauce has cooked down to a thick gravy.

3 Return the meatballs to the sauce and simmer uncovered for 10 minutes more. Carefully break the eggs into the sauce and poach for a few minutes (don't overcook the eggs). Serve at once.

SERVES 4

Spiced Lamb with Chermoula

PREPARATION 1 hr 30 mins **COOKING** 30 mins

4 cardamom pods
2 cloves
½ cinnamon stick
1 teaspoon cumin seeds
1 teaspoon coriander seeds
2 large cloves garlic
salt and freshly ground black pepper
1 lime, peeled and chopped
1 teaspoon olive oil
3 teaspoons pistachios
8 lamb cutlets

CHERMOULA

1 green capsicum
½ bunch mint
½ bunch coriander
2 cloves garlic
1 teaspoon ground cumin
1 teaspoon ground coriander
1 teaspoon paprika
½ teaspoon chilli powder
2 teaspoons salt
2 medium red onions
½ bunch flat-leaf parsley
¼ cup olive oil
2 tablespoons lemon juice

1 Pound cardamom, cloves, cinnamon, cumin and coriander in a mortar and pestle. Remove cardamom husks, add garlic, salt, pepper, lime, olive oil and pistachios and pound to a chunky consistency. Rub all over lamb and marinate for at least 1 hour.

2 Meanwhile, prepare the chermoula. Cook the capsicum under the grill or in the oven until the skin blisters. Remove skin under cold water and cut the capsicum flesh into strips. Place capsicum and all remaining ingredients in a food processor or blender and process to a thick paste and set aside.

3 Preheat oven to 180°C. Seal lamb in an oven pan on the stovetop, then transfer to the oven until just cooked, about 15–20 minutes for medium-rare. Let it rest for 5 minutes, then serve on steamed rice with chermoula piled on top.

SERVES 4

Spicy Lamb Tagine

PREPARATION 40 mins **COOKING** 1 hr 40 mins

500g lean diced lamb
2 onions, chopped
1 teaspoon ground cinnamon
½ teaspoon ground cloves
1 teaspoon garam masala
400g canned chopped tomatoes
2 cups beef stock
250g canned chickpeas, drained and rinsed
3 potatoes, chopped
2 carrots, chopped
45g sultanas
finely grated zest of ½ orange
3 teaspoons cornflour, blended with 1 tablespoon water

1 Heat a non-stick frying pan over a medium heat. Add lamb and cook, stirring, for 5 minutes or until lamb is brown. Remove lamb from pan and place in a tagine.

2 Add onions to pan and cook for 3 minutes, then add cinnamon, cloves and garam masala. Cook until spices are fragrant and onions are soft.

3 Add onion mixture, tomatoes, stock, chickpeas, potatoes, carrots, sultanas and orange zest to tagine and simmer for 75–90 minutes or until lamb is tender.

4 Stir cornflour mixture into lamb and cook for 5–10 minutes longer or until tagine thickens slightly. Serve with couscous.

SERVES 6

Veal Couscous Casserole

PREPARATION 35 mins **COOKING** 25 mins

¾ cup couscous
2 tablespoons oil
2 onions, sliced
½ teaspoon cardamom seeds
2 teaspoons brown mustard seeds
2 cinnamon sticks
4 dried curry leaves
500g minced veal
1 tablespoon tomato paste
400g canned chopped tomatoes
1 cup chicken stock
1 green capsicum, chopped
125g canned corn kernels, drained

1 Place couscous in heatproof bowl and cover with ¾ cup boiling water. Set aside for 10 minutes or until all liquid is absorbed.

2 Heat oil in a medium saucepan. Add onions, seeds, cinnamon and curry leaves and cook, stirring until onions soften and seeds begin to pop. Add veal and cook over high heat until veal is well browned. Mix in tomato paste, tomatoes and stock. Bring to the boil and simmer, uncovered, for 5 minutes.

3 Add capsicum, corn and couscous to saucepan, mix well to combine. Cover and simmer for 10 minutes. Remove the curry leaves before serving.

NOTE You can substitute lamb for the veal in this recipe, if you like.

Salads

Whatever the dish, there is usually a great deal of attention paid to the spices – subtle, rich blends that often include cinnamon, cumin, saffron, turmeric and ginger. Moroccan food isn't spicy hot in the way that, for example, Indian and Pakistani food often is, though these cuisines share many of the same flavours. Another star of Moroccan cuisine is produce – the fruits and vegetables of Morocco are some of the finest in the world.

SERVES 4–6

Diced Lemon and Onion Salad

PREPARATION 15 mins

3–4 fresh thin-skinned lemons
1 large red onion, diced
¾ cup flat-leaf parsley, coarsely chopped
½ teaspoon sugar
salt and freshly ground black pepper

1 Peel the lemons and remove the pith. Cut in half lengthwise, removing the core and seeds, and cut into 5mm dice.

2 Toss the lemon, onion, parsley and sugar together. Add salt to taste, place in serving bowl. Sprinkle lightly with ground black pepper and serve.

SERVES 4

Moroccan Eggplant Salad

PREPARATION 30 mins **COOKING** 25 mins

3 eggplants, chopped
1 medium onion, minced
2 cloves garlic, minced
1 tablespoon olive oil
4 small tomatoes, chopped
1 red capsicum, chopped
½ teaspoon freshly ground black pepper
½ teaspoon ground ginger
½ teaspoon turmeric
½ teaspoon ground cumin
3 tablespoons tomato paste
½ cup flat-leaf parsley, chopped

1 Put the eggplants on an open flame or under the griller until the skin is burned black. Put the eggplant in a plastic bag, rubbing briskly between the hands to remove the burned skin, then chop the flesh.

2 Sauté the onion and garlic in the olive oil over medium-high heat. When the onions have become soft, add the eggplants, tomatoes, capsicum and spices. When the tomatoes are soft, add the tomato paste, lower heat, cover and simmer for 15–20 minutes.

3 Allow to cool, sprinkle with chopped parsley and serve.

SERVES 4–6

Broad Bean Salad with Cumin Dressing

PREPARATION 20 mins **COOKING** 10 mins

500g frozen broad beans
1 small red onion, finely diced
3 tablespoons olive oil
2 tablespoons lemon juice
1 teaspoon ground cumin
¼ cup flat-leaf parsley, finely chopped
2 cloves garlic, finely chopped
salt and freshly ground black pepper

1 Place the frozen beans in boiling salted water and cook until tender, about 10 minutes. Drain, cool a little then remove outer skin.

2 Toss the beans and onion together in a salad bowl. Whisk remaining ingredients together and pour over the salad. Toss well and chill before serving.

SERVES 4–6

Spicy Carrot Salad

PREPARATION 40 mins COOKING 1 hr 20 mins

500g baby carrots
2 tablespoons olive oil
juice of 1 lemon
½ teaspoon chilli powder
1 teaspoon ground cinnamon
1 teaspoon sugar
1 clove garlic, crushed
1 teaspoon salt
½ teaspoon ground ginger

1 Place whole carrots in a saucepan, cover with water, bring to the boil and cook for about 20 minutes until soft. Leave them in their cooking water for about 1 hour.

2 When cool, strain the carrots and cut them into quarters lengthwise.

3 Return carrots to the pan, cover with the rest of the ingredients and heat for a few minutes to blend the flavours.

4 Leave to cool. Serve garnished with freshly chopped parsley.

SERVES 4

Eggplant and Capsicum Salad

PREPARATION 25 mins **COOKING** 15 mins

1 red capsicum
¼ cup olive oil
4 medium eggplants

DRESSING

3 tablespoons olive oil
2 tablespoons lemon juice or vinegar
2 cloves garlic, crushed
½ teaspoon paprika
¼ teaspoon cayenne pepper
¼ cup flat-leaf parsley, finely chopped

1 Slice off the 4 sides of the capsicum, trim off curved ends so pieces are flat. Brush or spray the skin side with oil. Grill under a hot grill skin-side up until skin has blistered. Remove to a plastic bag, stand for 15 minutes.

2 Remove stems from the eggplants. Peel off 1cm-wide strips of skin lengthwise at intervals, giving a striped effect. Slice into rounds 5mm thick. Set aside.

3 Brush or spray both sides of the eggplant with oil. Grill on both sides until browned and cooked through. Place attractively onto a serving platter. Skin the capsicum slices and cut into small dice. Sprinkle over the eggplant.

4 Whisk the dressing ingredients together and pour over the salad. Stand for 10 minutes before serving.

SERVES 4

Cucumber Salad with Mint

PREPARATION 15 mins

5 Lebanese cucumbers
¼ cup fresh mint, finely chopped
1 tablespoon lemon juice
⅓ cup vegetable oil
1 teaspoon orange flower water
1 teaspoon freshly ground black pepper
finely grated zest of 1 orange

1 Finely peel cucumbers and slice thinly. Put in a bowl and add the mint. Combine lemon juice, oil, orange flower water, pepper and orange zest in a small screw-top jar and shake well to combine.

2 Pour dressing over cucumber slices and mix well.

SERVES 6

Orange, Date and Walnut Salad

PREPARATION 15 mins

400g salad greens such as mignonette, coral or salad mix
3 medium oranges
50g fresh dates
50g walnuts, coarsely chopped

DRESSING

2 tablespoons lemon juice
½ teaspoon sugar
2 tablespoons light salad oil
salt and freshly ground black pepper

1 Wash the salad greens in cold water, drain and wrap in a clean kitchen towel. Place in the refrigerator for 1 hour or more to crisp.

2 Cut the skin from the oranges just past the pith line. Slice into 5mm rounds crosswise.

3 Remove pits and slice the dates lengthwise.

4 Arrange the salad greens on a platter and top with circles of overlapping orange slices. Sprinkle with the dates and chopped walnuts.

5 Whisk dressing ingredients together and drizzle over the salad.

SERVES 4–6

Beetroot Salad

PREPARATION 25 mins   COOKING 5 mins

125g unsalted butter, softened
½ teaspoon salt
½ teaspoon freshly ground black pepper
2 tablespoons balsamic vinegar
handful fresh oregano leaves, plus 8 sprigs finely chopped
handful fresh thyme
handful fresh basil leaves
2 green onions, chopped
1 red onion, chopped
6 bay leaves
1 tablespoon olive oil
4 large beetroot, cooked

1 In a heavy-based non-stick frying pan on high heat, melt the butter, add salt, pepper, balsamic vinegar and chopped oregano. Stir, turn off the heat and set aside.

2 In a glass bowl, put the fresh oregano, thyme and basil leaves, green onions, red onion and bay leaves.

3 Add olive oil to gloss the leaves and incorporate all the flavours, toss and add the beetroot. Put the salad on a plate, spoon the dressing around the plate, then over the salad.

4 Add a little more olive oil to the plate to give the salad a two-tone effect. Remove bay leaves and serve immediately as the dressing is hot.

SERVES 4–6

Orange and Date Dessert Salad

PREPARATION 10 mins

6 oranges
12 fresh dates
2 teaspoons orange flower water
1 teaspoon ground cinnamon

1 Peel oranges thickly, past the pith line. Cut into thin round slices with a sharp knife. Place on a platter in overlapping circles.

2 Remove the pits from the dates and slice thinly lengthwise. Sprinkle on the orange slices and drizzle all over with orange flower water. Dust with cinnamon passed through a fine sieve. Chill before serving. Garnish with fresh mint and serve with whipped cream or yoghurt.

SERVES 4

Moroccan Salad

PREPARATION 10 mins

1 green capsicum, deseeded
1 red capsicum, deseeded
2 medium tomatoes
1 Lebanese cucumber
1 small red onion
1 tablespoon olive oil
1 tablespoon balsamic vinegar
salt and freshly ground
black pepper
12 pitted black olives, chopped

1 Wash and peel the vegetables. Cut them into small dice then combine in a salad bowl.

2 Mix together oil, vinegar, salt and pepper. Pour the dressing over the salad and mix well. Garnish with black olives.

SERVES 4–6

Radish and Orange Salad

PREPARATION 10 mins

4 oranges
10 red radishes
⅓ cup fresh lemon juice
1 tablespoon sugar
pinch of salt

1 Peel the oranges with a sharp knife, removing all pith. Cut through the membrane on each side of the segment to release the segments.

2 Trim top and root end of the radishes and grate on a coarse grater.

3 Toss the orange segments and grated radish together in a salad bowl. Mix the lemon juice, sugar and salt together and pour over the salad, toss gently. Chill before serving.

Desserts

Moroccans usually eat fruit for dessert. A simple plate of prepared fresh fruit or dessert marks the end of the meal, before mint tea is served. This doesn't mean that sweets don't exist in Morocco, however – Moroccans have quite a sweet tooth and they don't hesitate to snack on heavy, cream-filled pastries between meals.

SERVES 4

Cornflour Pudding

PREPARATION 10 mins COOKING 10 mins

3 tablespoons cornflour
⅓ cup sugar
⅛ teaspoon salt
2 egg yolks
1 cup cold milk
1½ cups scalded milk
1 teaspoon vanilla extract

1 Mix cornflour, sugar and salt in a double boiler. Beat egg yolks with 2 tablespoons of the cold milk.

2 Add the remaining cold milk to the double boiler, then gradually add the scalded milk. Stir until thick. Add some of the mixture to the eggs, then add this back to the double boiler and cook for 5 minutes.

3 Remove from heat, add vanilla, stir well and serve in bowls, sprinkled with chopped pistachio nuts and cinnamon.

SERVES 4

Spiced Pears with Oranges and Caramel Sauce

PREPARATION 45 mins   COOKING 30 mins

4 medium pears each, peeled
¾ cup sugar
45g unsalted butter
¼ teaspoon ground cinnamon
¼ teaspoon ras-el-hanout*
2 oranges, sliced

1 Using a melon baller and starting from the bottom, core each pear. Cut a thin slice off the bottom of each pear to make level.

2 Stir sugar and ¼ cup water in a heavy-based large saucepan over medium heat until sugar dissolves. Increase heat and boil until syrup is deep amber colour, brushing down sides of pan with a wet pastry brush and swirling pan occasionally, for about 5 minutes.

3 Remove pan from heat, whisk in butter, then 2 tablespoons water.

4 Stand pears in caramel sauce in saucepan. Sprinkle over cinnamon. Cover and cook over low heat for 10 minutes. Uncover and sprinkle with ras-el-hanout. Cover and continue to cook until pears are tender, occasionally spooning caramel sauce over pears and shaking pan so pears don't stick, about 15 minutes.

5 Arrange orange slices around pears and spoon over caramel sauce. Cover and simmer until orange slices soften, about 5 minutes.

6 Place orange slices on plates. Stand pears on top of orange slices and spoon caramel sauce over. Serve warm or at room temperature.

---

* Ras-el-hanout is a popular blend of herbs and spices that is used across the Middle East and North Africa. The name means 'head of the shop' in Arabic, and refers to a mixture of the best spices a seller has to offer. There is no definitive set combination of spices that makes up ras el hanout.

SERVES 6

Date and Walnut Slice

PREPARATION 30 mins COOKING 25 mins

125g butter, chopped, at room temperature
¾ cup caster sugar
1 egg, lightly beaten
¾ cup chopped dried dates
½ cup walnuts, coarsely chopped
1 teaspoon ground ginger
1 cup self-raising flour

1 Preheat oven to 180°C. Grease a 20 x 20cm Swiss roll tin. Line base and two long sides with baking paper.

2 Place butter and sugar in a small bowl. Beat with an electric mixer until thick and creamy. Add egg, beat until just combined. Stir in remaining ingredients (except zest) until well combined. Spread mixture into prepared tin.

3 Cook for about 20 minutes or until cooked when tested. Cool slice in tin.

4 Remove slice from tin. Serve slice cut into bars.

MAKES 60–70

Ghoriba with Almonds

PREPARATION 40 mins COOKING 25 mins

7 eggs, beaten
250g sugar
7g yeast
zest of 1 lemon
1kg chopped almonds
200g semolina
orange blossom water
icing sugar

1 Preheat oven to 200°C. Mix the beaten eggs with the sugar, yeast and zest. Add the chopped almonds and the semolina little by little. Work this mixture energetically until it becomes a soft dough.

2 Dampen hands with orange blossom water, take walnut-size pieces of dough, roll into balls then flatten slightly.

3 Sprinkle icing sugar on a bench and place the flattened sides of the dough on the sugar. Arrange the balls on a greased baking tray with the sugary side on top.

4 Cook for 20–25 minutes. Remove from oven and allow to cool before storing in an air-tight container.

MAKES 20

Almond and Walnut Petits Fours

PREPARATION 35 mins   COOKING 15 mins

125g whole skinned almonds
125g walnuts
250g caster sugar
finely grated zest of ½ orange
2 medium egg whites
10 large glacé cherries, halved
1 tablespoon icing sugar

1 Preheat the oven to 180°C and line a baking sheet with rice paper.

2 Put the almonds and walnuts in a food processor and grind briefly. Add half the caster sugar and grind again until it becomes a powder.

3 Mix in the remaining caster sugar and the grated orange zest. Transfer the mixture to a bowl.

4 In another bowl, whisk the egg whites lightly with an electric whisk, then stir the egg whites into the almond and walnut mixture to bind it. Take heaped teaspoonfuls of the mixture and roll it into balls on a work surface dusted with icing sugar.

5 Flatten the balls with a palette knife and press half a cherry into the centre of each. Place them well apart on the baking sheet.

6 Bake for 15 minutes or until just firm but pale golden brown. Cool on the baking sheet then trim the rice paper around the biscuits.

7 Serve the petits fours on the day of baking, dusted with icing sugar.

MAKES 48

Almond Biscuits

PREPARATION 35 mins **COOKING** 15 mins

1 cup plain flour
1 cup ground almonds
¼ teaspoon baking powder
⅛ teaspoon salt
90g butter, softened
¾ cup sugar
1 large egg white
½ teaspoon almond extract
48 whole blanched almonds

1 Preheat oven to 180°C. Stir together flour, ground almonds, baking powder, and salt and set aside.

2 In a mixing bowl, cream butter and sugar with an electric mixer on medium. Beat in egg white and almond extract.

3 Stir flour and ground almond mixture into the creamed mixture. Cover with cling wrap and chill for about 2 hours.

4 Shape dough into small balls, about 4cm. Place balls 5cm apart and flatten slightly with the bottom of a glass. Press an almond into the centre of each biscuit. Bake for about 12 minutes, or until set but not browned.

SERVES 4

Almond Serpent Cake

PREPARATION 1 hr **COOKING** 50 mins

200g almond meal
100g icing sugar
1 egg white, lightly beaten
zest of 1 lemon
¼ teaspoon almond extract
1 tablespoon orange flower water or rose water
6 sheets filo pastry
60g unsalted clarified butter, melted
1 egg yolk, beaten with a little water
2 tablespoons icing sugar
½ teaspoon cinnamon

1 Preheat oven to 180°C. Place almond meal in a bowl and sift in the icing sugar. Add the beaten egg white, lemon zest, almond extract and orange flower water or rose water and mix into a firm pliable paste. Pat out into an even shape and cut into three even pieces.

2 Sprinkle work surface with icing sugar and roll 1 piece into a long sausage shape. Pinch along the sausage to make it 45cm long and 1cm thick. Repeat with the 2 remaining pieces. Line a 20cm round cake tin or flan tin with baking paper.

3 Place a sheet of filo on work surface, long side in front of you, and brush with melted clarified butter. Place a second sheet on top and brush with butter. Place 1 sausage of almond dough 5cm in from edge, fold filo over the almond roll and roll to the end, brush with butter, then form a coil and place in the centre of the prepared pan. Form two more filo almond rolls and continue the coil. Brush with egg yolk.

4 Bake for 30 minutes. Remove from oven, turn out onto an oven tray, remove paper and return to oven for 10–15 minutes until golden and crisp. Invert onto a wire rack to cool to warm. Slide onto a serving plate. Sieve icing sugar on top and sprinkle cinnamon around edge to form a border. Cut into wedges to serve.

MAKES 20–24

Deep-Fried Honey Puffs

PREPARATION 40 mins   COOKING 30 mins

3 eggs
¼ cup orange juice
¼ cup vegetable oil
zest of 1 large orange
¼ cup caster sugar
300g plain flour
2 teaspoons baking powder
vegetable oil for deep-frying

SYRUP

2 tablespoons lemon juice
1½ cups sugar
⅓ cup honey
zest of 1 large orange

1 Whisk together the eggs, orange juice and oil. Add the orange zest and sugar and whisk well.

2 Sift flour and baking powder together, stir into the egg mixture with a wooden spoon until thoroughly combined.

3 Sprinkle work surface with extra flour, turn out the dough. Knead lightly until smooth and roll out to 5mm thickness. Cut into round cakes with a 5cm biscuit cutter.

4 Place syrup ingredients in a saucepan with 1½ cups water, stir while it comes to the boil, turn down heat and simmer for 5–6 minutes. Set aside.

5 Heat oil to 170°C or until a 1cm cube of bread turns golden in 20 seconds. Add honey cakes a few at a time and fry until puffed and golden on both sides. Remove and drain on absorbent paper.

6 Place a few cakes at a time into the warm syrup, turn to coat, then remove to a serving dish with a slotted spoon. Serve immediately.

SERVES 6

Mint Tea

PREPARATION 5 mins COOKING 10 mins

1 tablespoon Chinese green tea
4 tablespoons sugar
½ cup fresh mint leaves

1 Rinse out the tea pot with boiling water. Add tea leaves, sugar and mint leaves.

2 Pour in 1 litre boiling water from a height to oxygenate the water. Cover with the lid and stand to infuse for 3–4 minutes. Serve immediately.

NOTE It is traditional to serve this mint tea in glasses. Garnish with a fresh mint sprig.

SERVES 4

Sweet Couscous with Nuts and Dried Fruits

PREPARATION 20 mins COOKING 10 mins

1 cup couscous
¼ cup caster sugar
pinch of salt
45g unsalted butter, cut into dice
½ cup dried apricots, cut into thin strips
5 pitted dates, quartered lengthwise
1 tablespoon raisins
1 tablespoon sultanas
50g blanched almonds, toasted
2 tablespoons pistachio nuts, coarsely chopped

FOR SERVING

2 tablespoons caster sugar
½ teaspoon cinnamon
1½ cups hot milk

1 Place the couscous in a large heatproof bowl and add 1 cups boiling water, the sugar and salt and stir until all water has been absorbed by couscous.

2 Cover and set aside for about 15 minutes. Fluff with a fork, then mix in the butter, fruit and almonds.

3 Pile into a suitable serving dish or platter in a conical shape. Sprinkle the pistachios on top.

4 To serve, combine sugar and cinnamon in a bowl and place on the table with a jug of hot milk. Each person helps themselves spooning couscous into individual bowls.

NOTE This is usually served as a snack at any time. It also makes a tasty breakfast dish. Leftovers may be covered and stored in the refrigerator then heated when needed in the microwave. Other combinations of dried fruits and nuts may also be used.

SERVES 4–6

Honey Almond Briouats

PREPARATION 45 mins COOKING 30 mins

350g marzipan
60g chopped almonds
½ teaspoon almond extract
¼ cup orange flower water
10 sheets filo pastry
90g butter, melted
1 cup honey

1 Preheat the oven to 180°C and line 2 oven trays with baking paper.

2 Mix together the marzipan, chopped almonds, almond extract and ¼ of the orange flower water.

3 Stack the filo sheets on a cutting board and cut into strips of about 10cm wide and 30cm long. Wrap the strips in a moistened kitchen towel and cover to keep from drying out.

4 Place one strip of filo on your work surface and brush with melted butter. Fold the strip in half lengthwise (making it about 5cm wide) and brush with butter again.

5 Place one teaspoon of the almond filling on one end of the strip and fold one corner over, making a triangle. Continue folding the triangle, enclosing your filling until you reach the end of the strip.

6 Fold all your strips this way and place on the oven trays. Brush the tops with melted butter. Bake on the middle shelf for 20–25 minutes until golden.

7 While the briouats are baking, put the honey and the remaining orange flower water in a saucepan. Bring to the boil right before the briouats come out of the oven. Reduce the heat of the pan and plunge the briouats into the hot honey mixture two at a time. Leave in for 10 seconds, then remove with a slotted spoon onto baking paper. Allow to cool before serving.

Index

This edition published in 2025 by New Holland Publishers

newhollandpublishers.com

A record of this book is held at the National Library of Australia.

ISBN 9781760797874

Food photography: Paul Nelson, Brent Parker Jones, R&R Photostudio (www.rrphotostudio.com.au) and New Holland Image Library
Food Stylists: Lee Blaylock, Michelle Finn, Rebecca Quinn
Recipe Development: R&R Test Kitchen

Managing Director: Fiona Schultz
General Manager/Publisher: Olga Dementiev
Designer: Andrew Davies
Production Director: Arlene Gippert
Printed in China

Keep up with New Holland Publishers:

NewHollandPublishers
@newhollandpublishers

US $19.99
UK £14.99